How Long Is God's? Nose?

Also by John Timmer

God of Weakness
The Kingdom Equation
Once Upon a Time . . .

How Long Is God's Nose?

AND 89 OTHER STORY SERMONS FOR CHILDREN

John Timmer

ZondervanPublishingHouse
Grand Rapids, Michigan

A Division of HarperCollinsPublishers

How Long Is God's Nose?
Copyright © 1997 by John Timmer

Requests for information should be addressed to:

📖 ZondervanPublishingHouse
Grand Rapids, Michigan 49530

Library of Congress Cataloging-in-Publication Data

Timmer, John, 1927–
    How long is God's nose : and 89 other story sermons for children / John
Timmer.
       p.   cm.
    ISBN: 0-310-20186-1
    1. Children's sermons.   I. Title.
BV4315.T54 1997
252'.53—dc20   96-40992
         CIP

Interior design by Jody DeNeef

Printed in the United States of America

---

97 98 99 00 01 02 03 04 /❖ DH/ 10 9 8 7 6 5 4 3 2 1

To my grandchildren
Sarah
Rachel
John
Libby
Matthew
and . . .

Contents

Introduction

How Long Is God's Nose? is a second collection of story sermons for children. Like the first collection, *Once Upon a Time . . .* (1992), these stories were originally told to children in a worship setting. A variety of genres are included—folk and fairy tales, legends, fantasies, historical anecdotes, personal experiences, and Bible stories. As they are presented here, they can be read by parents to their children, told by teachers to their students in a church school or Christian school setting, or used by pastors as children's sermons.

Some of the stories are my own. Others I have gathered from a variety of sources. As much as possible I have tried to give credit where credit is due; however, I have not been able to trace every story.

In preparing this manuscript my wife, Hazel, has been of invaluable editorial help. My special thanks to her.

The Mountain Dragon

Once, long ago and far away, there was a small village at the foot of a mountain. On this mountain lived a dragon.

When the dragon wagged its tail, tall trees came crashing down. When the dragon opened its mouth, fire came out. When the dragon sneezed, a strong wind blew.

The people in the village were very afraid of the dragon. They looked at the mountain and said, "What if the dragon comes down the mountain, enters our village, and wags its tail and spits fire? That will be the end of our village. And what if the dragon comes down during the night when it's dark?"

All these fearful questions kept the people in the village from sleeping well. They often heard things go bump in the night. "What's that noise?" they would ask. "Could that be the dragon?"

"No," someone would say, "that's just a couple of cats fighting over the garbage outside. Go to sleep."

Now in this village lived a little boy. One night this little boy had a dream. In this dream God told him what to do about the dragon.

The next morning the boy went to the village square. He told the people, "Last night I had a dream. In this dream God told me, 'Go up the mountain to where the dragon lives. Always keep your eyes on the dragon and never look back.'"

And that's what the boy did. He climbed the mountain, keeping his eyes on the dragon most of the time. Whenever he looked back at the village down below, he heard the dragon make the most terrible noises. But when he looked at the dragon again, the dragon was quiet.

When the boy came to where the dragon was, something strange happened. The closer he came to the dragon, the smaller the dragon became—until finally the dragon was about as big as the boy's hand. The boy reached down, grabbed the tiny dragon, put it in his pocket, and went back to the village and showed it to the people.

"Is that all?" the people asked. "Is that the dragon we were so afraid of?"

From that day on the people of the village were a lot happier and slept much better.

Doesn't that story remind you of the story of David and Goliath? The people of Israel were as afraid of Goliath as the people in the village were afraid of the dragon. Then David, who was just a boy, said, "What are you people so afraid of? Don't you believe that God is stronger than Goliath and can easily knock him down?" Then David took his slingshot and killed big Goliath with a small stone. After that the people were a lot happier and slept much better.

Who Does the Playing?

Once upon a time there was a father mouse and a mother mouse and their two children, Know-It-All and I-Know-Better. They lived inside a piano, where life was very quiet until one day, their whole world was suddenly filled with music. When the music stopped, Father Mouse said, "Wasn't that beautiful? Only God can make music like that." Mother Mouse and the two children agreed. They said, "Who else but God can make such beautiful music?"

Then one day, daughter Know-It-All came back from exploring the piano. She said, "God doesn't make the beautiful music we're hearing. Wires do. I saw wires inside the piano. They are the secret. When they tremble and vibrate, they make music."

Because Know-It-All was very smart, the others believed her. They no longer believed that God made the beautiful music. They believed that the wires did.

Then one day, son I-Know-Better came back from exploring the piano. Even though I-Know-Better was not as smart as his sister Know-It-All, he was no dummy. He always knew what he was talking about. "Guess what!" he told the family. "Wires don't make the music. Piano hammers do. Piano hammers are the secret. When they dance on the wires, they make the music."

"Well," Mother Mouse said, "then we'd better change what we believe." And that's what they did. They no longer

---

(Adapted from a story that appeared in the April 7, 1963, issue of *The Observer*.)

believed that the wires made the music. They believed that the piano hammers did.

Then one day, Father Mouse came back from exploring the piano. "Guess what!" he said. "Guess who makes all the music! Not the wires. Not the piano hammers. It's the woman who lives in this house! Through a tiny hole I saw her. I saw her hitting the outside of the piano with her two hands, and suddenly I heard beautiful music."

So once again, the mice changed what they believed. It was not God who made the music. It was not the wires. It was not the piano hammers. No, it was the woman who lived in the house.

That evening after the music had stopped, Know-It-All suddenly asked, "If the woman makes the piano hammers go and if the piano hammers make the wires go, I wonder what makes the woman go?"

That was a very good question. The mouse family talked about it for hours. Finally Mother Mouse said, "I think God does. I think God moves the woman to hit the outside of the piano so that beautiful music fills our world."

"You are right," the others said. And from then on the family of mice once again thanked God for all the beautiful music they heard.

Slivers

Have you ever had a sliver in your finger? If you have, then you know that slivers are no joke. I remember having a sliver in my right thumb when I was a little boy. I tried to pull it out but couldn't. It was in too deep.

So what do you think I did? Did I go to my mom and say, "I've got a sliver in my thumb. Can you please pull it out for me?" Oh no! I was afraid it would hurt too much, so I told no one.

After a couple of days the sliver began to cause an infection. My thumb began to throb. It became red and swollen. When I touched it, it hurt.

Still I didn't tell my mom. I told myself, "It will get better by itself." But it didn't. Instead of getting better it got worse.

After a while I couldn't grab hold of things anymore. You know, each time you pick up something you use your thumb.

Finally I told my mom. "We'll go see a doctor right away," she said.

And we did. I still remember what the doctor did. He took a good look at my thumb, picked up a pair of small scissors, and cut open my thumb.

I was dumbfounded. I thought, "How dare he? How dare he cut open my thumb?"

But he did. He cut open my thumb and cleaned up the infection.

A tiny sliver can cause a bad infection. You know what else can cause an infection? Being angry at someone for a long time. Anger is like a sliver in your finger. If you don't pull it out, it can give trouble—a lot of trouble.

So, if you are angry at your friend or your brother or your sister, get rid of the anger. Talk about what happened. Forgive. Become friends again. For if you don't, your anger will cause a bad infection. And infections are no joke.

The Hungry Whale

Once upon a time, so a Russian story goes, there lived a whale. The people of a fishing village caught the whale. Because it was hungry, the villagers fed the whale. The whale ate everything they fed it but still was hungry. The people brought more food. Again the whale ate all the food but still was hungry.

In time, the villagers ran out of food, so they brought the whale to a neighboring village. Here the same thing happened. The people gave the whale all the food they had, but the whale was always hungry.

The people loved the whale very much, and they wanted to keep it. If only they could feed it enough. They asked the whale, "What will it take to fill you?"

The whale answered, "Food, food, and still more food. I'm always hungry."

"But we've given you all the food we have," the people said.

"Even if you give me a thousand times more food," the whale said, "I will still be hungry."

"Then what is it you really want?" the people asked.

The whale answered, "God! What I really want is God. As long as I don't have God, I will be hungry."

That was a smart whale. The whale knew what many people don't. It knew that as long as we don't have God, we will never be satisfied and will always want more and more and still more.

Jesus told a story about always wanting more. Once upon a time, he said, there was a man who always wanted more and more things. When he got them, he put them in a big barn and never looked at them again. When the barn was full, he built another barn, and then still another and another and another.

Then one night God came down and talked to him. God said, "You fool! Look at all the junk you have. Barns full of things. But one thing you don't have. You don't have me. And because you don't have me, you will always be hungry."

Wisdom

Once upon a time there was a rich man who had two sons. One day he told his sons, "Listen carefully. I'm a rich man. But I'm also an old man. I'm going to die very soon and have decided not to divide my money between you. My money will go to one of you—the one who passes a test. This is what I want you to do. After I die, you must both jump on your horses and ride to the nearest village. The one whose horse arrives in the village last will get all my money. But the one whose horse arrives in the village first will get nothing."

Soon after the father had spoken these words, he died. The two sons did what their father had told them. They jumped on their horses and began riding to the nearest village. But the closer to the village they came, the slower they rode, for each wanted his horse to arrive last. Finally they were hardly moving at all.

They said to each other, "This is silly. If we keep on riding this slowly, neither of us will ever get to the village. Why don't we visit a wise man and ask him what we should do?"

So that's what they did. They went to a wise man and told him what their father had said before he died. The wise man listened to their story. Then he said, "Bend over and I'll whisper my advice in your ears."

So the two brothers bent over. No sooner had the wise man whispered his advice than the brothers ran outside, jumped on the two horses, and rode to the village as fast as they could.

My question is, What advice did the wise man whisper? Do you want to know? Well, he told the brothers to switch horses. For remember the father's words: "He whose horse arrives last will get all my money." Because each brother wanted his own horse to arrive last, each galloped off to try to arrive first on his brother's horse.

I hope you will remember this story. Every once in a while, like the two brothers, you'll get in a fix, too, and simply won't know what to do. What you need then is wisdom—wisdom from someone who is much wiser than you are. Wisdom from people like your mom or dad.

Wild Kitten

Once a mother and her two children went for a ride. Suddenly the children began shouting, "Mom, stop the car! Go back! There's a kitten on the side of the road."

"So there's a kitten back there on the side of the road," the mother said. "We decided to go for a ride, remember? And going for a ride means that we can't stop for every animal we see on the side of the road. If we stop to pick up every animal, we'll end up with a zoo, and I'll end up being a zookeeper. No, thank you!"

"But you must pick up the kitten," the children said. "If you don't, it will die. And you don't want it to die, do you, Mom?"

"Well, then, it will just have to die," the mother said. "We simply don't have room for another animal. We already have two turtles, three dogs, and four cats."

"Oh, Mom, how can you be so mean to that poor little kitten? Let's turn around and take it home," the children pleaded.

"All right, all right. You children win," the mother said. She turned the car around and drove back to where the kitten was. "You kids stay in the car," she said to the children, "while I pick it up."

As she came close to the kitten, she saw that it was just skin and bones and that its eyes were runny. The kitten was

---

(Adapted from Fred B. Craddock, "Praying through Clenched Teeth," in James W. Cox, ed. The Twentieth-Century Pulpit, vol. 2 [Nashville: Abingdon, 1981], 51f.)

also scared and mean. When she reached out, it hissed and scratched her hand. She grabbed the kitten by the skin of its neck, carried it to the car, and warned the children, "Leave it alone! Don't touch it! It's wild and probably has fleas. It's probably sick, too."

When they got home, the children gave the kitten three baths. Then they gave it more milk than you drink for breakfast every morning. They fixed a warm place for it to sleep.

Several weeks passed. Then one day the mother felt something rubbing against her leg. She looked and saw it was the kitten. Reaching down, she stroked it. This time the kitten did not hiss and scratch. It purred.

God is like that mother, and we are like that wild kitten. We hiss at God. We scratch God's hand. We say, "Leave us alone. We don't need you."

But God picks us up anyway, takes us home, and feeds and cares for us.

The story of the kitten is our story. It explains what we do to God. It explains what God does to us.

Are You Looking for a Pet?

Are you looking for a pet? If you are, let me give you some advice. Don't get a walrus.

You may ask, "Why not? What's wrong with having a walrus for a pet?"

You want to know? Okay, then let me ask you a couple of questions. Do you have any idea how much a walrus weighs? About 2000 pounds. And do you have any idea how much a walrus eats? About 100 pounds of food a day. And do you know what a walrus likes to eat the best? Shellfish. A walrus eats thousands of shellfish every day. It eats the meat inside the shells and then spits out the empty shells, thousands of them every day. You can imagine the terrible mess that makes.

"Well," you say, "that's no problem. My mom or dad can clean up that mess."

Okay, so empty shells are no problem, but what about a place to keep the walrus? Have you thought about that? To keep a walrus, you need more than a regular swimming pool. You need a very deep swimming pool, for a walrus likes to swim in water that is 300 feet deep.

You should also know that a walrus doesn't like to swim alone. A walrus likes to swim in groups of 200 to 300 walruses. And that, I think, would be too much for you to handle. You would need a swimming pool as large as the city block you live on and a truckload of food every day.

"Okay," you say, "I'd better not ask my mom or dad for a

(Inspired by William L. Coleman, *Singing Penguins and Puffed-up Toads*, [Minneapolis: Bethany House, 1981], 27–29).

walrus. Clearly God didn't make walruses to be pets. But why did God make walruses?"

God made walruses for the people who live in the far north, where there's always snow and ice. They eat walrus meat, make ropes out of walrus muscles, make spoons out of walrus tusks, and even use walrus whiskers for toothpicks. They don't kill or capture walruses just for fun. They use every part of the walrus.

So take my advice. If you're looking for a pet, don't get a walrus.

Plastic Bags

Many years ago our family lived in Japan, where we were missionaries. The first house we lived in wasn't built too well. If we were sitting in the living room, for example, we could see the sky through a crack in the wall. And the roof leaked in many places, as we found out one rainy night.

We had gone to bed, and soon we were sound asleep. Then something woke me up, something wet on my face. I tried hard to ignore it and go back to sleep, but I couldn't. Every couple of seconds I felt a wet spray on my face. I discovered that rainwater was dripping from the ceiling onto the windowsill right next to my face.

I woke up my wife. We moved the bed, put a cloth on the windowsill to catch the drip, and went back to sleep.

After a while my wife woke me up. "It's dripping on my side of the bed," she said. We moved the bed again, put a pan under the drip, and went back to sleep.

After a while I woke up. This time water was dripping from the ceiling on my side of the bed. But this time there was no escape. The bedroom was small, and there was no place left to move the bed away from the drips. Then we had an idea. We pinned plastic bags to the ceiling—one bag over each drip to catch the rainwater. And we went back to sleep.

The next morning when I opened my eyes and looked up at the ceiling, guess what I saw? Plastic bags with rainwater in them!

I had thanked God for many things, but never for plastic bags. That morning I did thank God for plastic bags.

Sometimes God helps us see everyday things in a new way. Can you thank God for something you use every day?

Honor Your Father and Mother

Once upon a time there was an old man, so old that his hands trembled. When he ate, his fork or spoon sometimes missed his mouth, and often he spilled food on the tablecloth.

The old man lived with his son and his wife, who found the old man's eating habits disgusting. "Cleaning up the mess takes so much time," they said. "You'd better eat in a corner of the kitchen. Come right here behind the stove."

So each time they ate, they made the old man sit all by himself behind the kitchen stove and served him food in a clay bowl. One day the bowl dropped from his trembling hands and broke. His daughter-in-law lost her temper. "If you act like a pig," she told the old man, "you must eat like a pig." So she bought a cheap wooden bowl. From that day on, he ate all his meals from a wooden bowl.

Now the woman and her husband had a four-year-old son. Some days later they noticed that their son was playing with pieces of wood. "What are you doing, Son?" the father asked.

"I am making a trough," he said.

"A trough?" the father asked. "What for?"

"For you, Mom and Dad. You can eat from it when you get to be as old as Grandpa."

The man and woman looked at each other, dumbstruck. They didn't know what to say. They cried a little. And then they brought the old man back to the table, put him in a comfortable chair, and gave him food on a plate. From then on they never got angry at the old man when he spilled his food.

(Adapted from the Brothers Grimm story, "The Old Man and His Grandson.")

Warts and All

ong, long ago, in a faraway country, there lived a
Lprincess who was very beautiful. She was so beautiful, she was almost perfect. I say *almost* perfect because there
was one thing the matter with her—one tiny thing. On the
tip of her beautiful nose there was a tiny wart.

One day her father the king talked to her. He said,
"You're old enough to marry a handsome prince. I have
found such a handsome prince for you. Next month he will
come to the palace and marry you. I promise you that it will
be the most beautiful wedding the world has ever seen."

This made the princess very happy, and she could hardly
wait to meet her handsome prince.

Finally the day arrived. The prince entered the palace and
bowed low to greet the princess. But then, when he looked
at the princess's face, he had the shock of his life. For there,
at the tip of her beautiful nose was that tiny wart.

"No one ever told me about the wart," the prince said.
"I'm sorry, but I can't marry a princess with a wart on her
nose. I simply can't." And he turned around, walked out of
the palace, and went back to his own country without marrying the princess.

Well, you can imagine how the poor princess felt. She felt
just terrible.

"Does having a wart on the tip of my nose mean I can
never marry a handsome prince?" she cried.

A year went by. Again the king talked to his daughter

(Adapted from John Aurelio, *Story Sunday* [New York: Paulist Press,
1978], 9–16.)

about marrying. "I have found a handsome prince who wants to marry you," the king said.

"But did you tell him about the wart on my nose?" the princess asked. "Yes, I did," the king assured her. "The prince said the wart makes no difference."

And it didn't. When the prince first saw the princess, can you guess what he did? He kissed her right on her nose. Then, when the princess looked at the handsome face of the prince, she had the shock of her life. For what she saw was a wart on the tip of the prince's nose.

You understand this story, don't you? All of us, you might say, have warts on our noses. All of us have things the matter with us. Therefore, none of us can say, "I don't like that girl because she has funny hair," or "I don't like that boy because he talks too much." We must love others, "warts and all," and always remember our own warts.

The Stonecutter

One of my favorite stories is the story of the stonecutter. It's a very old story, so you may have heard it before. But listen to it again and you may like it even more.

Long ago in a country called Japan there was a stonecutter. He worked hard each day cutting stones from rocks. He earned very little. One day, as he was working with his hammer and chisel in the hot sun, he said, "I wish I were rich and lived in a big house."

No sooner had he said this than the miracle happened. He turned into a rich man who lived in a big house. How happy he was, but not for very long. For one day he saw the king go by. He was riding in a chariot surrounded by many soldiers and pulled by many horses.

Oh, how I wish I were a king, the stonecutter thought, *for no one is mightier than a king.*

No sooner had he thought this than the miracle happened. He turned into a king sitting in a carriage surrounded by many soldiers and pulled by many horses.

But the sun was hot and burned his face. The king looked at the sun and said, "You are more powerful than I am. How I wish I were the sun."

No sooner had he said this than the miracle happened. He turned into the sun and shone on the earth.

Suddenly a big cloud moved between the sun and the earth, so that the rays of the sun could no longer warm the earth. "That cloud is mightier than I am," the sun said. "It keeps me from warming the earth. How I wish I were that big cloud."

No sooner had the sun said this than the miracle happened. The sun turned into a big cloud. The cloud shed rain on the earth, so much rain that the rivers overflowed and swept away everything in their paths. Everything except one big rock. That one big rock did not move no matter how hard it rained.

This made the cloud furious. It shouted, "That rock is mightier than I am. Oh, how I wish I were that rock." And again the miracle happened. Suddenly the cloud turned into that rock. How happy the rock was.

But not for long, for one day there came a stonecutter who cut pieces out of the rock. This made the rock furious. It shouted, "That stonecutter is mightier than I am. I wish I were that stonecutter."

And the miracle happened one more time. Suddenly the rock turned into the stonecutter.

Now here's a question for you: Who, do you think, is that stonecutter? That stonecutter is you and I. Sometimes we look at other people and feel jealous of them. Sometimes we look at others and say, "I wish I were that boy or that girl— she's so smart or he's so strong." When we say things like that, we are just like the stonecutter. Then we're trying to be what we are not. Be content with what you are, and thank God for making you *you*.

Lloyd and Muriel

Missionaries are interesting people. Many of them are real characters. Like, for example, Lloyd and Muriel. Lloyd and Muriel were Lutheran missionaries I knew in Tokyo, Japan, many years ago. They had five children—and not much money.

They had a sign that you could see when you entered their house. It said:

Use it up!
Wear it out!
Make it do!

And that's what they did. They used everything up, wore everything out, and made everything do.

In winter it always was cold in their house. The cold didn't bother them, for they wore several layers of clothing. But it bothered the people who visited them.

Every once in a while a group of us missionaries would meet in their home. After a while we all would start looking at the thermostat and rubbing our hands. Then Muriel would say to Lloyd, "Lloyd, I think our guests are cold. Why don't you turn the heat up a little bit?" And then Lloyd would turn up the heat from 50 to 55 degrees. At least, that's what it felt like.

Down the street from Lloyd and Muriel's home, there was a store that sold fresh fruit and vegetables. Boxes of not-so-fresh fruit and vegetables stood around the back of the store, waiting to be dumped as garbage. Now it so happened that Lloyd and Muriel had a goat from whose milk they made cheese. One day Muriel asked the store owner, "May we please have the old fruit and vegetables for our goat?"

"Sure," the man said, "help yourself."

So Muriel began feeding the store's leftovers to the goat. But after a while she thought, *This stuff doesn't look half bad. In fact, it's still good enough for my family to eat.* So that's what her family ate.

During dinner one day, one of their children said, "You know, Mom, we must be the only family in Japan that eats garbage."

Lloyd and Muriel are retired now. I haven't seen them for a long time. Just thinking about them makes me want to see them again. They're such interesting people. Such characters. I wish you could meet them, too. Maybe you will someday in heaven. When you meet them, tell them: "Lloyd and Muriel, being in heaven sure beats eating garbage, doesn't it?" And then watch them laugh.

God Loves All Colors

Once upon a time, not so long ago, in a place not very far away, on one side of a small town, lived a people whom everybody called "the Greens." They lived in green houses, wore green clothes, ate green food, drank green water, and went to green churches where they worshiped a green god. Their children went to green schools, played with green toys, and slept in green beds.

On the other side of town there lived a people whom everybody called "the Blues." They lived in blue houses, wore blue clothes, ate blue food, drank blue water, and went to blue churches where they worshiped a blue god. Their children went to blue schools, played with blue toys, and slept in blue beds.

The Greens and the Blues had nothing to do with each other. They never spoke to each other. They just didn't like each other. Green parents taught their children to say:

Green is lucky;
Blue is yucky.
Greens are glad;
Blues are sad.

Blue parents taught their children to say the exact opposite:

Blue is lucky;
Green is yucky.
Blues are glad;
Greens are sad.

(Adapted from Lawrence Castagnola, *Parables for Little People* [Saratoga: Resource Publications, 1982], 15–18.)

This went on for many years. Never once were the Greens and the Blues kind to each other. Never once did they speak to each other or do things together. They completely ignored each other.

Then, one day, a man walked into town. This man was a friend of children, of all children, whether they were green or blue. He went around blessing all the children in town. And the strange thing was that each time he blessed green children, they turned blue, and each time he blessed blue children, they turned green.

At first the parents of the green and blue children were very upset about this. But after a while they said, "Even though our children changed color, they are still our children and we still love them." Green parents said, "We love our children, even if they are blue." And blue parents said, "We love our children, even if they are green."

And so it happened that green people came to like blue people and that blue people came to like green people. So it happened that blue and green people taught their children to sing:

Green is good, but so is blue.
Red and yellow, black and white are too.
All the children should be glad;
There's no color that is bad.

Gentle As an Elephant

Do you know who Hannibal was? Hannibal was an army general who lived before Jesus was born. He was one of the greatest generals that ever lived.

Hannibal did something unusual: He used elephants in his army. Today generals use tanks, but in Hannibal's time there were no tanks. Hannibal used elephants instead. His soldiers built small fortresses on top of the elephants. From inside these fortresses they shot arrows at the enemy below.

But using elephants has one problem: Whenever storms arise, elephants may stampede. They may panic and start to run.

So what do you think Hannibal did to keep his elephants from stampeding during storms? He ordered his soldiers to tie live chickens to the elephants' feet. Why? Because elephants are such gentle animals, they would never step on the live chickens. Even during bad storms, Hannibal's elephants didn't move, afraid to step on the chickens tied to their feet.

Elephants are big and strong. Yet there is much gentleness in them. Who put that gentleness there? God did, when he created them. When God created elephants, he said, "When people see these big animals, it will scare the daylights out of them. I'd better put some extra gentleness in them, so people won't be afraid of them."

Some people are so gentle that others say of them, "They wouldn't hurt a fly." Well, elephants are so gentle, they wouldn't hurt a chicken. That's good to know, don't you think?

Fish Hawks

A fish hawk is a bird. So is a pelican. Fish hawks and pelicans are both birds that like to eat fish. But now listen carefully to how these birds catch their fish.

The fish hawk circles in the sky, waiting and watching for a pelican to scoop a fish out of the water in its big bill. At the moment a pelican makes the catch, the fish hawk comes swooping down making horrible noises. The pelican looks up in surprise as if to ask, "Who's making all that racket?"

It opens its mouth. Then the fish hawk quickly snatches the fish out of the pelican's mouth and flies off to enjoy a fish dinner.

This catching and stealing business has been going on for thousands of years. A pelican catches a fish. A fish hawk comes swooping down, screeching at the top of its lungs. The pelican looks up and opens its mouth.

And the fish hawk steals the fish and flies off with it.

You can't help but wonder: Don't those pelicans ever learn their lesson? Don't they ever learn to ignore the screeching noises of the fish hawk? Don't they ever learn to keep their mouths shut after catching a fish? And don't the mother and father pelicans ever teach their children never to trust a fish hawk? Don't they ever tell their children, "When you hear that awful sound overhead, don't look up and don't open your mouth, because a fish hawk is trying to steal the fish you just caught"?

But no, each time fish hawks screech, pelicans are foolish enough to look up and open their mouths.

Isn't it funny the way God made those two birds? The one catches the fish; the other steals and eats it. That arrangement would never work in your family, would it? Let's say your sister is about to eat a cookie. You yell and quickly take it away from her and put it in your mouth. The moment you do that, you'll be in trouble, deep trouble. Your sister and your mom or dad won't let you get away with it. So you don't even try. But the bird world is different. The fish hawk does get away with it. Why? Because God made the bird world different from the people world.

That a pelican catches a fish and a fish hawk snatches it away and eats it is very funny—I think. It shows that God has a sense of humor. What do you think?

Thermometer or Thermostat?

In your home you can find these two things: a thermometer and a thermostat. This is how they differ: A thermometer simply tells you what the temperature is. When you have a fever, your mom or dad might stick a thermometer in your mouth, look at it after a while, and say, "Oh-oh, you have a temperature of 104." A couple of hours later they might put the thermometer in your mouth again and then say, "Oh, good, your temperature has gone down to 100."

A thermometer simply records the temperature. It doesn't change the temperature. But a thermostat is different. A thermostat doesn't just record the temperature, it also changes it. For example, when it is cold in the house, your mom or dad turns up the thermostat. The thermostat turns on the furnace, and the furnace heats up the house.

A thermometer records the temperature, and a thermostat changes the temperature.

Which one do you think Jesus is like? A thermometer or a thermostat? If you said "thermostat," you are right.

Jesus is like a thermostat because he changes things. For example, one day Jesus visited the temple in Jerusalem, saw all the money changers, and kicked them out of the temple. If Jesus had acted like a thermometer, he would have said, "Look at all those money changers. They're turning the temple into a bank. Instead of worshiping God, they're making money. How terrible!" And Jesus would have walked away and not done a thing.

Instead, Jesus acted like a thermostat. He changed things.

He knocked over the tables of the money changers and drove them out of the temple.

Followers of Jesus do the same thing. When they see a bad situation, they don't just say, "How terrible!" They act like thermostats and try to change the situation.

Counting Legs

You have heard of Abraham Lincoln, haven't you? Abraham Lincoln was the president of the United States some 130 years ago.

One day a group of people came to visit Lincoln. He talked with them for a while, and then he asked them this question, "How many legs would a sheep have if you called its tail a leg?"

All the visitors said, "Five, Mr. President. If you called its tail a leg, a sheep would have five legs."

"Not so," said Lincoln. "A sheep would still have four legs, as many legs as God gave it when he created it. A tail remains a tail, no matter what you call it. Calling a tail a leg does not change it into a leg."

Let me put it this way. On my left wrist I wear a watch and on my nose I wear glasses. Now, how many watches would I be wearing if I called my glasses a watch? One, of course. I would still be wearing only one watch. For my glasses remain glasses no matter what I call them.

How many ears do you have? Two. Right? You have two ears. Now, how many ears would you have if you called your nose an ear? Three ears? Of course not. You would still have two ears, for your nose remains a nose no matter what you call it.

The reason I told you the story about Abraham Lincoln is that many people believe what Lincoln said isn't true. Many people believe that if they give something wrong a different name, they change it into something right. They might steal something and then say that they found it. "It was just lying there, so I took it." Or they might lie and then say, "I was only helping a friend stay out of trouble."

You see what's happening? Sometimes we call an ugly thing by a pretty name and believe in that way we can turn the ugly thing into a pretty thing. But stealing is stealing, no matter what you call it. And lying is lying, no matter what you call it. And a tail is a tail, no matter what you call it.

How many legs would a sheep have if you called its tail a leg?

Jesus and Soap

Two men went for a walk. One was a minister and the other was a soapmaker. The soapmaker did a lot of talking. The minister did a lot of listening.

The soapmaker said to the minister, "Tell me, what good is the church? What good are all your sermons? What good is the Bible? What good is Jesus? Look at all the trouble in the world. People fight. People steal. People kill. People hate. The church has been here for two thousand years. Sermons have been preached for two thousand years. People have read the Bible for two thousand years. People have believed in Jesus for two thousand years. Have things gotten any better? People still do what they did two thousand years ago. They still fight and steal and kill and hate."

The minister said nothing. He just listened. After a while they came to a place where children were playing in a mud puddle. The minister said to the soapmaker, "You say that soap makes people clean? I don't believe it. Look at those children. See how dirty they are? What good is soap? Soap has been in the world for thousands of years. But even with all the soap in the world those children are still covered with mud."

The soapmaker said, "But Pastor, soap does no good unless people use it."

"Exactly," the minister said. "Soap does no good unless people use it. What is true of soap is true also of Jesus. Jesus does no good unless people use him—unless people do what Jesus tells them."

A Hiding Place

When I was a little boy, I lived in a three-story house. My bedroom was on the third floor, right beneath the roof. From my bedroom window I could look down on our neighbor's two-story house.

One day from my window I noticed something. I saw a bird building a nest right behind the eaves trough. And I wondered, "Why is the bird building a nest right there? Why that little spot?"

Then it dawned on me. *Of course,* I thought, *behind the eaves trough the nest is well hidden. No one can do the bird any harm, not even the neighborhood cats.*

A couple of weeks later I noticed little birds in the nest. Once I saw the mother bird spread her wings and the little birds hide beneath them. *What a warm and safe place that must be,* I thought.

A couple of years later something happened that made me remember that scene. War had broken out in the country where I was living. It was Sunday afternoon. We had come home from church. My mom had prepared dinner. We were all sitting around the dinner table. Suddenly air-raid sirens warned that enemy planes were approaching our city. I thought to myself, *This is the end. The end of me. The end of my family. Pretty soon bombs will drop and destroy our house and kill us.* I dropped my fork and sat there frozen in fear.

Then my dad said, "Let's go stand in the hallway. They say it's the safest place in the house."

So we all moved to the hallway. My heart was pounding. I was terrified.

"Why don't we pray? That's the only thing we can do," my dad said. And he prayed that God would protect us. "Lord," he prayed, "cover us with your wings so that nothing will harm us." When he prayed that, I thought of those little birds and the mother bird covering them with her wings.

When we hide under God's wings, we are safe. When we hide under God's wings, nothing can harm us. Not really.

Three Trees

I once read a story about three trees.

Long, long ago, in a faraway forest, so the story goes, three trees were growing up together. One day they talked about what they would like to be when they grew up.

The first tree said, "I would like to be part of a beautiful home where many famous people come and admire my wood."

The second tree said, "I would like to be the mast of a big ship that people admire and that sails to faraway countries."

And the third tree said, "I would like to be part of a high tower—a tower so high that people will come from all over the world to admire it."

After many years, the three trees were cut down. The first tree didn't become part of a beautiful home, as it had hoped. Instead, some of its wood was used to make a manger—the manger in which Mary laid baby Jesus.

The second tree didn't become the mast of a big ship, as it had hoped. Instead, its wood was used to make a fishing boat—the boat that carried Jesus across the Sea of Galilee.

The third tree didn't become a high tower, as it had hoped. Instead, its wood was used to make the cross on which Jesus suffered and died.

It's a beautiful story. Also a very deep story. You'll need the rest of your life to understand it.

(Adapted from *The Tale of Three Trees* by Angela Elwell [Batavia, Ill.: Lion, 1989].)

Sloths

Do you know what a sloth is? A sloth is an animal. A strange-looking animal. When I look at a sloth, I say to myself, *Am I glad I'm not a sloth!*

Of course, a sloth may think the same thing about me. A sloth may think, *Am I glad I'm not a human being!* I guess what you think of others depends on who or what you are. But since I am a human being and not a sloth, I think sloths are strange looking.

A sloth has almost no tail and no ears and a blunt nose. A sloth doesn't have five toes as you and I do. Some sloths only have two toes, while others have three. Sloths are slow-moving animals that live in trees.

But by far the strangest thing about a sloth is that it is an upside-down animal. If you want to look a sloth straight in the eye, you have to turn your head upside down. Sloths live upside down. They eat upside down. They walk upside down. They even sleep upside down, hanging from tree branches. Sloths spend their whole lives living upside down in trees.

That doesn't sound very exciting, does it? Who would like to live that way? Who would like to walk upside down, eat upside down, and sleep upside down?

Yet strangely enough, this is what many people do. They live upside down. Not really, of course. They don't walk on their hands or eat hanging upside down from the kitchen ceiling. But they live upside down in another way: They don't live the way Jesus wants them to live.

Let me explain. Jesus says that we must seek God first. He says we must make God number one in life and ourselves number two. He says that when we do that, we're living right side up. But many of us do just the opposite. We make ourselves number one and God number two. And that's living upside down. That's turning Jesus' words on their head. That's living like a sloth.

The next time you go to the zoo and see the upside-down sloths, think about this story and say to yourself, "Sloths definitely are not my kind of animal!"

Augustine

Do you know who Augustine was? Have you ever heard his name? If you haven't, listen to my story.

Augustine lived sixteen hundred years ago. He lived in North Africa, close to the Mediterranean Sea. Augustine was a great thinker, a great Christian thinker. He thought about God a lot and wrote many books about God.

One day Augustine was walking along the beach of the Mediterranean Sea. He noticed a boy playing in the sand, pouring seawater into a hole. The boy would scoop up water from the sea with his hands, walk over to the hole he had dug, and pour the water into the hole. Then he would go back to the sea for more water.

Augustine watched the boy for a while and then asked him what he was doing. The boy said, "I'm pouring the Mediterranean Sea into my hole."

Augustine said, "Little boy, you're wasting your time. You can never do it. You can never pour the sea into your little hole."

But the boy, who knew who Augustine was, said, "Well, Mr. Augustine, then you're wasting your time, too. For you're writing books about God. You're trying to pour God into your books. You can never do that."

Smart boy! He understood that God is like the sea—God is as wide as the sea and God is as deep as the sea. There is so much of God that we can never say enough about him. There is so much of God that we can never hear enough about him. That's why we go to church Sunday after Sunday to hear a little more about the God who is wider and deeper than the sea.

Giving Wisely

Long ago in a faraway place there was a woodcutter. The woodcutter was walking around in a forest looking for something.

All the trees in the forest were watching the woodcutter. They wondered, "What is he looking for?" Finally one of the trees asked him, "Mr. Woodcutter, it seems that you are looking for something. Can I be of help to you?"

"As a matter of fact, you can," said the woodcutter. "I'm looking for a piece of tough wood. You see, the handle of my ax is broken and I need a new ax handle. What I'm looking for is a piece of wood tough enough for a new handle."

"Well," the tree said, "I'm made of tough wood. You may have one of my branches."

The woodcutter thanked the tree, cut off one of its branches, and fitted it into his ax. But as soon as he had fixed his ax, what do you think the woodcutter did? He chopped down the tree that had given him the branch.

As the tree fell down, it spoke these words: "Before you give, make sure you give wisely."

Giving things to people who do bad things with them is not giving wisely. I once did that. When I was in the army, someone asked me, "Will you give me some money? I need it badly." So I gave him some money. But what do you think he did with it? He got drunk with it. He got drunk with my money.

The Bible says that if someone is hungry, give her bread to eat. If someone is thirsty, give him water to drink. That's giving wisely. But if you give money to someone who gets drunk with it, that's giving unwisely. So the tree was right. Before you give, make sure you give wisely.

The Tenth Apple

Once upon a time there was a woman who had nothing. And I mean nothing, absolutely nothing. Because she had no food, God gave her food. God gave her three apples. So the woman ate the apples. She ate apple one and apple two and apple three.

And because the woman had no shelter from the sun and the rain, God gave the woman another three apples to trade for shelter. So the woman traded the apples. She traded apple four and apple five and apple six for shelter from the sun and the rain.

And because the woman didn't have any clothes, God gave the woman three more apples to trade for clothes. So the woman traded the apples. She traded apple seven and apple eight and apple nine for clothes to cover her body.

Finally, God gave the woman one more apple—apple ten—so the woman would have something to give to God. By giving the apple back to God, she would be saying, "Thank you, God, for giving me nine apples."

The woman looked at the tenth apple and admired it. It seemed larger and juicier than the other nine apples. The tenth apple looked so good that the woman ate it. Then she handed the apple core back to God.

Many of us do the same thing. We eat the tenth apple and hand the core back to God.

God gives us ten cents. Nine cents we may use for our-

(Adapted from W. J. Bausch, *More Telling Stories, Compelling Stories* [Mystic: Twenty-Third, 1993], 79.)

selves. But the tenth cent God expects us to give back to him. God gives us ten dollars. Nine dollars we may use for ourselves. But the tenth dollar God expects us to give back to him. God gives each of us ten apples. Nine apples we may use for ourselves, for food, shelter, clothes, and other needs. But the tenth apple God expects us to give back to him.

Is that fair? What do you think?

The Alphabet Prayer

One of my favorite stories is one that I read many years ago. It's about a woodcutter. The woodcutter had a prayer book full of prayers. Each night before he went to bed, he prayed a prayer from the prayer book.

One day he was working as usual in the forest. He worked hard all day. Evening came, and the woodcutter decided to sleep in the forest.

When it was time to go to sleep, the woodcutter realized that he had forgotten his prayer book. What should he do? The woodcutter didn't know any prayers by heart. So this is what he prayed:

Dear Lord,

I am a simple man. I am also a little forgetful, forgetful enough to have forgotten my prayer book. What is worse, I don't know any prayers by heart. But you, O Lord, know all the prayers, even before I say them. So this is what I'll do: I will say all the letters of the alphabet. As I say them, please make a prayer out of them.

Then the woodcutter said all the letters of the alphabet: a, b, c, d, e, f, g, h, i, j, k, l, m, n, o, p, q, r, s, t, u, v, w, x, y, z.

And God, who hears our prayers, took all the letters, all twenty-six of them, and made them into a most beautiful prayer.

Are You Superstitious?

Are you superstitious? Maybe you're thinking, *Maybe I am and maybe I am not—I don't know what the word* superstitious *means.*

Let me explain. Are you afraid to walk under a ladder because you believe that when you walk under a ladder something bad will happen to you? If you believe that, you are superstitious.

Or maybe you believe that when a black cat crosses your path something bad will happen to you—unless you spit in the road or cross your arms or take nine steps backward or go home and start all over. If you believe that, you are superstitious.

Or, if you are a girl, do you believe that if a butterfly lands on you, you'll get a new dress? Or you'll get a new dress if you catch the first butterfly in spring and bite off its head? If you believe either of those, you are superstitious.

Or maybe you believe that when you have to take a test at school, you must do one of the following things to pass the test:

- Wear your socks and underwear inside out.
- Carry a dogtooth in your pocket.
- Step on every crack in the sidewalk on your way to school.
- Cross your legs while taking the test.
- Swallow a live goldfish beforehand.

If you believe things like that, you are superstitious.

Are Christians superstitious? We shouldn't be. Because being a Christian means believing that God takes care of us everywhere—even while walking under or standing on top of ladders. Being a Christian means believing that God keeps watch over us day and night.

Dirt

Dirt. What is it? Dirt is good stuff in the wrong place. Dirt is good stuff in a place where it shouldn't be. Take milk, for example. Milk in the right place is good stuff. Milk in a glass is milk in the right place. But milk in the wrong place is dirt. Milk on your pants or skirt is dirt. If you spill milk on your pants or on your skirt, your mom or dad will say, "It's dirty. You'd better throw it in the wash."

Or take jam. Jam in the right place is good stuff. Jam on toast tastes good. But jam in the wrong place is dirt. Jam in your hair is dirt. If you have jam in your hair, your mom or dad will say, "Your hair is dirty. You'd better shampoo it."

Or take oil. Oil in the right place is good stuff. Oil in a car engine is oil in the right place. But oil in the wrong place is dirt. Oil on the living-room carpet is dirt. If you spill oil on the living-room carpet, your mom or dad will say, "The carpet is dirty. We'd better call someone to clean it."

Or take money. Money in the right place is good stuff. Money you worked for is good money. But money in the wrong place is dirt. Money you stole from someone is dirt.

Or take words. Words in the right place are good words. Words like *God* or *Jesus,* when used in the right place, are good words. But words in the wrong place are dirt. Words like *God* or *Jesus* used as swear words are dirt. That's why God said, "Never use my name in the wrong place. Never treat my name like dirt. Always use it in the right place."

Henmi San

Some time ago I counted the number of times I have moved from one house to another. I counted twenty times.

I'm quite sure that when you are as old as I am now, you too will have moved many times. And each time you move, you'll leave friends behind. Many of them you will never see or hear from again. That's the sad part about moving: leaving friends behind.

Let me tell you about one friend whom I never saw or heard from after I moved away from Japan. Her name is Henmi San. I met her when I was a missionary in Japan. I had a Bible class for student nurses at a hospital near our home, and Henmi San was one of the nurses in my class. She was a Buddhist, not a Christian. But she showed great interest in Jesus because he traveled around healing people.

After Henmi San finished nursing school, I asked her, "What are you going to do?"

"I'm going to India to work among people who have leprosy," she answered.

"Before you leave," I said, "I would like to give you a Bible."

"All I'm taking with me to India is what can fit in my backpack. And it's already so full, I'm afraid there's no room for a Bible."

"After you get to India, send me your address. I'll send you a Bible," I offered.

Half a year later Henmi sent me a letter. "Dear Mr.

Timmer," she wrote, "I would very much like to receive the Bible you promised to send me."

So I sent her a Bible. But I never heard from her again. I don't know whether she became a Christian or not. I hope she did.

Whenever Henmi San's name pops into my mind, I say a prayer for her. I ask God to bless Henmi San's work as a nurse and to lead her to become a disciple of Jesus.

Each time you move, you'll leave friends behind. Many of them you'll never see or hear from again. But every once in a while the name of a friend you left behind will pop into your mind. When it does, say a prayer for your friend.

An Eye for an Eye

Some time ago I watched an old movie in which Stan and Ollie are selling Christmas trees. They have a truckload of Christmas trees and are going door to door.

Things are going just fine until they come to the house of a grouchy man. "I don't want a Christmas tree," he says. Bam! He slams the door shut in their faces.

But a branch of the Christmas tree gets caught in the door. So Ollie rings the doorbell again.

"You again?" the grouchy man growls. "I told you I don't want a Christmas tree."

As Stan begins to explain about the branch caught in the door, the man slams the door shut. This time the door catches Stan's coat. So Stan rings the doorbell again. "I'm terribly sorry," he says, "but my coat got caught in the door."

Again the man slams the door shut and once again a branch gets caught in the door. Again Stan and Ollie ring the bell.

This time when the grouchy man opens the door he has clippers in his hand, and he cuts up the tree.

Stan says, "I don't think he wants a tree."

But Ollie becomes so angry that he rips out the doorbell. And then when the grouch picks up the telephone to call the police, Ollie cuts the telephone wire.

From then on, things go from bad to worse. The grouchy man destroys Stan and Ollie's trees, one by one. He goes on to destroy their truck. Meanwhile, Stan and Ollie are destroying the man's house.

The Bible calls this way of acting "an eye for an eye, a

tooth for a tooth." You give me a black eye? I'll give you a black eye. You knock my tooth out? I'll knock your tooth out.

Jesus says, "Quit it! Quit that an-eye-for-an-eye and a-tooth-for-a-tooth business. That's no way to behave. I'll tell you how I want you to behave. When someone hits you, don't hit back. When someone kicks you, don't kick back. When someone hates you, don't hate back. Instead, pray for the person who hates you. That's how I want you to behave."

Ants, Mice, and Spiders

It was the week before Christmas, and I was sitting in my study, working on my Christmas Day sermon. Suddenly I noticed some ants walking across my desk. There were twelve of them. I looked at the ants, and right away I sensed that something special was going on. And there was, for these twelve ants made a circle.

As I was wondering what this might mean, I next saw three small mice walking across my desk. They were not the three blind mice out of the Mother Goose book. They were not blind, and they knew exactly where they were going—to the inside of the circle made by the twelve ants.

The twelve ants and three mice looked up. So did I. And guess what? From the ceiling came down a big spider that landed in the middle of the mice and the ants. This big spider did all the talking.

He said, "Reverend Timmer, the last couple of years at Christmastime, you have been telling stories to the children at church—stories about the stable where Jesus was born. Right?"

I said, "That's right!"

"And in these stories you talked about cows and sheep and chickens and horses and donkeys, and how they all kneeled before the baby Jesus. Right?"

I said, "That's right!"

"But do you know that we were there too? We too kneeled before the baby Jesus. But because we're so little, no one noticed we were there. But we were, and we want you to know that. Could you tell this to the children at church?"

I said, "I promise I will."

"Thank you," the spider said. "Thank you very much indeed."

Then the spider pulled itself up and disappeared above the ceiling, and the three mice and the twelve ants walked off my desk and disappeared behind the wall.

After they were gone I wondered, *Was I dreaming? Did I fall asleep and dream about twelve ants, three mice, and a spider? Or were they really here?*

Well, it doesn't matter, does it? Just so we remember that ants and mice and spiders, too, were in the stable on the night when Jesus was born.

Hollow People

Old MacDonald had a farm. And on that farm he had some trees. There was a big tree here and a small tree there. Here a tree, there a tree, everywhere a tree. But of all the trees on his farm, one tree was bigger and more beautiful than all the other trees. Its branches spread in all directions and offered cool shade to animals and people whenever the sun was hot.

All the neighbors were jealous of Old MacDonald for having such a tree. Whenever they drove past his farm, they would say, "Isn't that a beauty? If only we had a tree like that on our farm."

Then one day as Old MacDonald was watching a squirrel climb up the trunk of his favorite tree, he noticed that the squirrel disappeared into a hole.

"That's funny," Old MacDonald said, "I didn't know the tree had a hole in it. I thought the tree was solid all the way through. I'd better take a look."

When he did, he discovered that the tree was hollow. Old MacDonald knew that in the next storm a strong wind could blow his beautiful tree down.

When you grow up, you'll discover that many people are like Old MacDonald's tree. They may look strong on the outside, but they are hollow on the inside. They're hollow because they aren't filled with the Holy Spirit.

"Be filled with the Holy Spirit," the Bible warns. If you aren't, you're as hollow as Old MacDonald's beautiful tree.

Two Seas

In the country where Jesus lived there are two seas. The one is called the Sea of Galilee. Its water is blue. It's full of fish. Along its shoreline are many trees. Many birds live near it. Children play in the water. And for miles around, farmers use its water to grow crops.

The Sea of Galilee receives its water from a river in the north and gives its water to a river in the south.

The other sea is called the Dead Sea. Its water is murky and undrinkable. No fish swim in its water. No trees grow on its shoreline. No birds can be heard nearby.

The Dead Sea receives its water from the river in the north. But it doesn't give its water to any river in the south. It's the stingiest sea in the world. It tries to keep all the water it receives.

But the sun won't let it. The sun won't let the Dead Sea keep all the water it receives. The sun shines on the sea and takes away its water.

The difference between the Sea of Galilee and the Dead Sea is this: The Sea of Galilee receives its water and gives it away. The Dead Sea receives its water and keeps it. The Sea of Galilee is alive. The Dead Sea is dead.

There are two kinds of people in the world: Sea-of-Galilee people and Dead-Sea people. Sea-of-Galilee people receive and give away. Dead-Sea people receive and keep. Sea-of-Galilee people are alive. Dead-Sea people are dead.

Sleeping

How many hours do you sleep each day? About eight hours? A day has twenty-four hours. Of those twenty-four hours, you probably sleep at least eight hours. This means that you spend one out of every three hours in bed. It means that if you live to be ninety years old, you will have spent thirty years in bed, sleeping. That's hard to believe, but it's true.

Sleep is a mysterious thing. One moment we're awake; the next moment we're asleep. One moment we know where we are; the next moment we don't know anything. One moment we see our mom or dad standing next to our bed. The next moment we don't. Sleep is a mysterious thing.

Have you ever jumped into a deep hole? Going to sleep is something like that. You don't know what's going to happen. The hole may be deep. Then again, it may be shallow. You don't know because you can't see. You'll jump into the hole only if someone you trust says to you, "It's okay! It's safe! Don't worry! I'll be watching you!" Then you dare to jump.

Going to sleep is like that. It's like jumping into the unknown after someone has said to us, "It's okay. It's safe. I'll be watching you."

But who is saying those words? God is. God says:

"I never sleep.
I never sleep so that I can watch over all the children
who go to sleep every night;
who sleep eight hours a day;
who sleep one out of every three hours.
I never sleep so that all the children may safely sleep."

The Hamway Family

Once upon a time there was a family by the name of Hamway. Not Amway, but Hamway. Their name was Hamway because on Sunday they always ate ham.

One Sunday, as they were eating ham, Mr. Hamway said to Mrs. Hamway, "Why is it that before you cook a ham, you always cut off both ends of the ham? You've been doing this for as long as I can remember. Why?"

"The reason I do that," Mrs. Hamway said, "is because my mother always does that. Before she cooks a ham, she always cuts off both ends of the ham."

The next Sunday when Mrs. Hamway's mother was over for dinner, Mr. Hamway asked her, "Why is it that before you cook a ham, you always cut off both ends of the ham?"

"The reason I do that," she said, "is because my mother always does that. Before she cooks a ham, she always cuts off both ends of the ham."

The next Sunday, when Mrs. Hamway's grandmother was over for dinner, Mr. Hamway asked her, "Grandma, why is it that before you cook a ham you always cut off both ends of the ham?"

"The reason I do that," she said, "is because my mother always used to do that. Before she cooked a ham, she always cut off both ends of the ham."

Now it so happened that Mrs. Hamway's great-grandmother was still living. So Mr. Hamway went to visit her and asked, "Why is it that before you cooked a ham, you always cut off both ends of the ham?"

"I did that," she answered, "because when my husband

and I were first married we didn't have a pan big enough to hold a whole ham. And we were too poor to buy a bigger pan. So before a ham would fit in my small pan, I first had to cut off both ends."

Mrs. Hamway's great-grandmother had a good reason for cutting off both ends of the ham. All the others did not. They just copied what they saw, without thinking.

We do this sort of thing all the time. I'll give you two examples. Who wears earrings? Women do. Women have worn earrings for as long as we can remember. But, one day, someone asked, "Why? Why should only women wear earrings?" And people answered, "Women wear earrings because their mothers and grandmothers wore earrings." But because that is not a good reason, some men now wear earrings.

Another example. For many years black children in our country went to one school and white children went to another school. Black and white children did not go to the same school, until someone asked, "Why? Why should black and white children go to different schools? Why can't they go to the same school?" And people answered, "Black and white children have always gone to different schools." But because that is not a good reason, many black and white children now go to the same school.

When you don't understand why you're doing something, ask your mom or dad to explain. If they can't give you a good answer, ask your grandma or grandpa. If they can't give you a good answer, then maybe it's time for you to talk to your parents about doing things differently.

The Diamond Dipper

Do you know what a dipper is? A dipper is a cup with a long handle.

And do you know that there is a dipper up in the sky? It's a group of stars shaped like a long-handled cup. It's called the Big Dipper. Remember this as you listen to my story.

Once upon a time there was a little girl who lived in a country where the weather turned so hot that all the rivers and lakes dried up and the people were dying of thirst.

One day the girl went out into the woods and asked God to fill her dipper with water so her mother wouldn't die of thirst. Then she lay down and fell asleep. When she woke up, she found that her dipper was filled with water.

On the way home she stopped to pour a few drops of water into the mouth of a thirsty frog. The moment she did, the dipper in her hand changed to silver.

When she came home, she handed the silver dipper to her mother. But her mother said, "It's too late. I'm going to die. Give the water to someone who will live." The mother handed the dipper back to her daughter. The moment she did, the dipper changed to gold.

After a little while a stranger knocked at the door and begged for water. The girl handed him the gold dipper with water. As the stranger took it, the dipper changed to shining diamonds.

After he drank the water, the stranger said, "Blessed are

(Adapted from G. B. Hallock, *Three Hundred Five-Minute Sermons for Children* [New York: Harper, 1928], 206f.)

you, little girl, for I was thirsty and you gave me to drink." Then the stranger disappeared and the diamond dipper rose into the sky to shine among the millions of stars as the Big Dipper.

Tonight, if there are no clouds, go outside and ask you mom or dad to show you where the Big Dipper is. After you have found it, think of the story I just told you.

The Chicken Eagle

Once upon a time there was a man who was always looking down. "If I keep looking down long enough," he said, "I'm bound to find something." And he did. He found pennies and nickels and buttons—lots of buttons.

Then one day he found something he'd never found before—an eagle's egg. How the egg got to be in the place where he found it, no one could explain. Maybe a mother eagle had landed there and said to herself, *If I'm ever to get where I'm going, I'd better get rid of my egg. It's so heavy, it's slowing me down.*

Of course, that's just a guess. But there it was—an eagle's egg. And the man who was always looking down found it and carried it home and put it in the nest of one of his chickens. One day, out came a baby eagle.

This baby eagle grew up with the baby chicks. And because she grew up with them, she began acting like them. She learned to scratch the dirt like a chicken, to cluck like a chicken, and to cackle like a chicken. She learned to flap her wings and fly a few feet in the air like a chicken. But she never learned to soar up into the sky like an eagle.

Years went by. By now the eagle had grown old. Then one day she spotted a beautiful bird high up in the air floating with the wind. The eagle thought, *Wow! How wonderful! To be so free must be exciting. Poor old me. I'm just a dirt scratcher.* And the old eagle asked one of the chickens, "What kind of bird is that—that one there, way up in the sky?"

"That," said the chicken, "is an eagle. Eagles belong to the sky. We chickens belong to the dirt."

My question is: Which would you rather be like? Like a chicken or like an eagle? Would you rather scratch dirt or fly high? Would you rather look down at the black dirt or look up at the blue sky?

The Greatest

Once upon a time there was a thimble—a small cup worn on a finger to protect it from pricks while sewing—and this thimble said, "No one is bigger than I am. I am the greatest."

"Pardon me," said the bucket to the thimble, "but I am much bigger than you are. I am the greatest."

"Pardon me," said the barrel to the bucket, "but I am much bigger than you are. I am the greatest."

"Pardon me," said the pond to the barrel, "but I am much bigger than you are. I am the greatest."

"Pardon me," said the lake to the pond, "but I am much bigger than you are. I am the greatest."

"Pardon me," said the ocean to the lake, "but I am much bigger than you are. I am the greatest."

"Pardon me," said the earth to the ocean, "but I am much bigger than you are. I am the greatest."

"Pardon me," said the sun to the earth, "but I am much bigger than you are. I am the greatest."

"Pardon me," said the Milky Way to the sun, "but I am much, much bigger than you are. I am the greatest."

"Pardon me," said the universe to the Milky Way, "but I am much, much bigger than you are. I am the greatest."

"Pardon me," God said to the universe, "but you are no bigger than a thimble on my finger." And after God said that, there was silence. No one spoke. No one said, "Pardon me, God, but I am bigger than you are. I am the greatest." I wonder why no one said that. Do you know why?

(Adapted from John R. Aurelio, *Fables for God's People* [New York: Crossroad, 1988], 34f.)

Just Wondering

Do you ever wonder why things are the way they are? For example, why do you have two eyes and not three eyes? Two eyes in front and one eye in back. With an eye in the back you could keep an eye on what's going on behind you. Do you ever wonder about things like that?

Do you ever wonder why you have two ears and one mouth? Why not two mouths and one ear? Is it because God wants you to listen more and to speak less?

Do you ever wonder why spiders can walk up the wall and across the ceiling? Wouldn't it be neat if you could too?

Do you ever wonder why you become ornery and hard to live with when you get bored? "Johnny, stop pestering your sister!" your mom will say. "What's the matter with you?" And you answer, "I'm bored. I don't know what to do."

When a dog gets bored, what does it do? It goes to sleep. Now why didn't God make you more like a dog? Then every time you got bored you could go to sleep. It would make your mom a lot happier. It would also make your sister a lot happier.

And do you ever wonder why God made the sky blue and not green? "Ugh!" you say. "Imagine the sky being green. It would make me sick!"

But what if the sky were green and always had been green? Then you wouldn't know any better. Then if someone would ask, "Why isn't the sky blue?" you would say, "Are you crazy? What's wrong with the sky being green?"

Do you ever wonder about things like that? I'm just wondering.

Money

Have you ever heard the story of Dave? Even though Dave was only ten years old, he always thought about money. One morning, when he came down for breakfast, he put a card on his mother's plate.

When his mother saw it, she could hardly believe her eyes.

The card said:

Mother owes Dave:
$2.00 for running errands
$2.00 for cleaning his room
$4.00 for mowing the lawn
$2.00 for baby-sitting Mary
Total amount Mother owes Dave: $10.00

After Dave's mom read the card, she didn't say a thing.

The next morning there was a card on Dave's plate. And on top of the card was a ten-dollar bill. Dave picked up the ten dollar bill and was pleased.

Mm, he thought, *I'm a pretty good businessman.*

Then he read the card. It said:

Dave owes Mother:
$0.00 for three meals a day
$0.00 for clothes, shoes, toys
$0.00 for a beautiful room
$0.00 for picking up the mess he leaves every day
Total amount Dave owes Mom: $0.00

What do you think Dave did with the ten-dollar bill? If you had been Dave, what would you have done?

Tommy Tittlemouse

One Sunday night I went back to church to get my reading glasses. I had left them on the pulpit and I needed them. As I was looking for the glasses, I saw something move. It was a mouse.

"Hi there!" I said.

And the mouse said, "Hi!"

"What's your name?" I asked.

The mouse said, "My first name is Tommy and my last name is Tittlemouse. Tommy Tittlemouse."

"Don't tell me you're Tommy Tittlemouse out of the Mother Goose book!"

And Tommy said, "No, that's not who I am. That's my great-grandfather. I grew up in the fields. I'm a field mouse."

I asked, "Then why are you living in this church? Why did you become a church mouse?"

"For two reasons," Tommy said. "My first reason is that I like to hear you read from the Bible. Last week, for example, you read these words: 'I would rather be a mouse in the house of the Lord than run around with wild field mice.' Or something like that. When I heard those words, I said to myself, *Tommy, you're doing the right thing. You're a wise mouse because you live in God's house. The Bible is right. It's better to be a mouse in God's house than a field mouse.*

"And what is your second reason for living in this church building?" I asked.

"My second reason," Tommy said, "is that this is a cat-free building. I hate cats. Cats are mean. Cats are sneaky. Have you ever looked at their feet? They walk on soft little cushions.

They walk so softly, you never hear them come. Then, all of a sudden, down comes a paw, and POW! You're dead before you know it. I tell you, Pastor Timmer, being a mouse is no fun. We mice never know whether we'll be alive or dead in the next moment. Why did God make cats anyway? It just doesn't seem right."

"Listen Tommy," I said. "There're lots of things in the world that don't seem right—things like cats eating mice and foxes eating chickens and wolves eating lambs. But one day God is going to change all that. In the Bible it says that one day the wolf will live with the lamb, and animals won't hurt each other anymore. I think that means that one day the fox will live with the chicken and one day the cat will live with the mouse—not eat the mouse, but live with the mouse."

When I told Tommy this, his mouth dropped open and he said, "That's hard to believe."

"I know it is," I said, "but it's in the Bible. And if the Bible says that day will come, it will."

"I guess so," Tommy said, and then he ran off and disappeared into the darkness.

The Good Field Mouse

This week I had another talk with Tommy Tittle-mouse. I said, "You really hate cats, don't you?"

"I sure do," Tommy said. "All mice do. To us, the only good cat is a dead cat."

"I'm going to tell you a story," I said.

"I'm listening," Tommy said.

This is the story I told Tommy. A certain cat was walking down a lonely road when she met a couple of wild dogs who chased her and bit her and threw her up in the air and hurt her so badly that the dogs thought she was dead. So they left her. But the cat was not dead. She was only half dead.

After a while a house mouse came down the road and saw the cat lying there. The house mouse thought that the cat was dead and passed by on the other side of the road.

After a while a church mouse came down the road and saw the cat lying there. The church mouse thought, *That cat is not dead. She is only playing dead. If I come close to her, POW! her paw will come down, and she will grab me and eat me.* So the church mouse, too, passed by on the other side of the road.

After a while a field mouse came down the road. He saw the cat and felt sorry for her. He quickly ran off and found some other field mice. Together they dragged the cat to a shady place, where they cleaned her wounds and put medicine on them. They gave her water to drink and food to eat.

Then I asked Tommy, "Which of these three mice did the right thing? The house mouse, the church mouse, or the field mouse?"

Tommy said, "The mouse who helped the cat."
"Tommy, do as the field mouse did."
"Maybe," Tommy said. Then he scampered away.

Tommy and Jonah

Yesterday when I opened the church door, I almost stepped on Tommy Tittlemouse. "Tommy," I said, "you look as though you've gone through the wringer. What happened to you?"

"I had a Jonah experience," Tommy answered.

"A Jonah experience?" I asked. "What do you mean?"

"What I mean," Tommy said, "is an experience like the one you told about in a sermon some time ago. Remember you told how Jonah was swallowed by a big fish and how Jonah prayed in the belly of the fish and how God made the fish spit Jonah up?"

"Don't tell me you were swallowed by a fish," I said.

"Not by a fish. By a cat!" Tommy said. "Last week Wednesday morning I came out of my hole and just as I was thinking, *It's nice to live in a cat-free building*, POW! before I knew it, a cat grabbed me, stuck me in its mouth, and swallowed me alive. Down I went, down a dark tunnel. I couldn't see a thing. Then I landed in the cat's stomach. It smelled terrible. Everything felt wet and slimy and slippery. I was scared. I thought, *This is the end of Tommy Tittlemouse.*

"Then what happened?" I asked.

"Then I remembered the sermon you preached on Jonah. So I did what Jonah did. I folded my two front paws and prayed, 'God of Jonah, please save me from dying inside a cat.'"

"And what then?" I asked.

"Then the cat burped and burped and burped again. Before I knew it, I was flying through the air. I was out of the cat's stomach, out of the cat's mouth. As soon as I hit the floor, I ran for my hole."

"And that's the end of the story?" I asked.

"No. Then I said, 'God of Jonah, thank you for saving my life.' And after I said that, I took a bath, for I smelled as bad as the inside of a cat's stomach. But, boy, am I happy that I knew the story of Jonah. If I hadn't known that story, I'd now be part of that cat."

Harvest Stuff

One day when Tommy Tittlemouse and I were sharing a piece of cheese, I said, "Tommy, tell me something about your life."

"I was born and raised in a wheat field," he said. "My mom and dad were field mice. I loved my home—the smell of wheat, the open air, the silence, the peace. There were no people there and no cars. And there was plenty to eat. And plenty of space to play hide-and-squeak. You couldn't ask for a better place to live."

"Why didn't you stay there?" I asked. "Why did you leave the field? Why did you become a church mouse?"

"Because of the harvest," Tommy said. "At harvesttime big machines moved into our wheat field. They made a lot of noise. They mowed down all the wheat. They killed a lot of mice. At harvesttime we discovered that the field and the wheat didn't belong to us but to the farmer. We didn't know that. And that came as a big surprise to us."

"Lots of people live just like field mice," I told Tommy. "They think this world belongs to them. They think they can do whatever they want with it. They live as though there is never going to be a harvest. But they are wrong—just as you mice were wrong. One day there's going to be a harvest. One day Jesus is going to come. And when he does, we'd better be ready."

"Yeah!" Tommy said. "That's one reason I became a church mouse. To find out about all that harvest stuff." He swallowed the last bit of cheese and said, "See you later, and thanks for the cheese."

Three Blinded Mice

The next time I went to see Tommy Tittlemouse, I brought along a book of Mother Goose rhymes. "Tommy," I said, "there's a Mother Goose rhyme I'd like to read to you." And this is what I read:

Three blind mice, three blind mice,
See how they run, see how they run.
They all ran after the farmer's wife,
Who cut off their tails with a carving knife.
Did you ever see such a sight in your life
As three blind mice?

"I don't understand that nursery rhyme," I told Tommy.

"No wonder you don't," he said. "That nursery rhyme has got it all wrong. That's not what happened. I'll tell you what happened.

"One evening the farmer's wife heard a noise in the kitchen. The noise came from the kitchen counter. Quickly she grabbed a flashlight, tiptoed into the kitchen, and turned on the light. What she saw was three mice. They ran away as fast as they could, but because the light of the flashlight had blinded them, they couldn't see where they were going.

"Meanwhile the farmer's wife had grabbed a carving knife and began slashing away at the mice. Fortunately she didn't kill any of them, only cut off their tails, which is bad enough. So the nursery rhyme should read like this:

Three blinded mice, three blinded mice,
See how they run, see how they run.
They all ran away from the farmer's wife,

Who chopped off their tails with a carving knife.
Did you ever see such a sight in your life
As three blinded mice?

"All mice know this rhyme," Tommy said. "They learn it in mouse schools all over the country. We call it the 'Three Blinded Mice' rhyme. It shows how cruel people are. Even though we mice don't do people any harm, they do us harm. They're always trying to kill us. They put out mouse traps. They put out mouse poison. Why? Didn't God create us too? Then why kill what God created?"

After saying this, Tommy quietly left. And all week long I've been thinking about this question: Why kill mice that God created? I hope you will think about that question too.

Tommy's Christmas Story

"Tommy Tittlemouse," I called into the dark church, "where are you?"

"I'm right here," he said as he came crawling out of the pulpit Bible.

"What were you doing in the Bible?" I asked.

"Reading the Christmas story," he said.

"Can you tell me the story?" I asked.

"I sure can," he said. And this is what Tommy told me.

"Many, many years ago, Mary and Joseph were living in Egypt. They wanted to go to Bethlehem so Mary could have her baby there. But wicked Pharaoh wouldn't let them. So God spoke to Pharaoh. He said, 'Because you won't let Joseph and Mary go to Bethlehem, I will send so many mice that they will cover the entire land of Egypt. There will be mice everywhere—in your fields and in your houses and even in your beds.'

"And so it happened. God sent so many mice that wicked Pharaoh finally said, 'Okay, I will let Joseph and Mary go to Bethlehem.'

"Now as Joseph and Mary traveled from Egypt to Bethlehem, they fell into the hands of robbers who stole all their money and beat Joseph and went away, leaving Joseph half dead. But Mary they did not touch.

"After a while the Queen of Sheba came along. She invited Joseph and Mary into her carriage. She bandaged Joseph's wounds, pouring oil and wine on them. The Queen of Sheba dropped off Joseph and Mary at an inn. But there was no room for them in the inn. So they kept walking until they met three wise men who told them to follow a bright star. They followed the star, and it led them to Bethlehem. There Mary gave birth to baby Jesus.

"So you see that we mice had something to do with Christmas. We made wicked Pharaoh change his mind. If it hadn't been for us mice, Joseph and Mary would never have gotten to Bethlehem."

"Tommy," I said, "let me tell you something. What you've just told me is a lot of Bible stories all mixed together. If you want to know the true Christmas story, ask any of the children here in church. They know the true story and would love to tell it to you. So why don't you ask one of them?"

"Maybe I will and maybe I won't," Tommy said, as he ran off into the darkness—the darkness of his great ignorance of the Christmas story.

Hickory Dickory Dock

Tommy Tittlemouse, I found out, was an expert on Mother Goose rhymes. He knew and loved them all. One day I caught him standing on the top of an organ pipe, reciting this old favorite:

Hickory dickory dock,
The mouse ran up the clock.
The clock struck one,
The mouse ran down,
Hickory dickory dock.

I clapped in appreciation but then asked, "What is this rhyme all about?"

"It's about mouse heroes," Tommy said. "You see, Mr. Dock—whose first name was Hickory, whose middle name was Dickory, and whose full name was Hickory Dickory Dock—was a great enemy. Mr. Dock is dead now, but when he was still alive he was a fierce enemy. He set mousetraps all over the house. He put poisoned food in every corner. And he had a couple of mean cats. So living in Mr. Dock's house was very dangerous. Some of the mice there got eaten by his cats, others died of eating poisoned food, and quite a few were caught in his traps. They were so afraid that they hardly dared leave their holes. What they needed was a hero, someone who would stand up to Mr. Dock. What they needed was a hero mouse who dared to run up Mr. Dock's clock and wait for it to strike. For when the clock struck, Mr. Dock would always look at the clock and say, 'Is it that late already?'

"As I said, what those mice needed was a hero mouse

who would dare to run up the clock, wait till the clock struck the first time, wait till Mr. Dock looked at the clock and saw the hero mouse, who would then stick out her tongue and say, 'Ah ha ha ha haaaaah ha!' Then she would run down the clock before it struck the second time and make it back to her hole before a cat caught her.

"To do that took a lot of courage. Usually not more than one mouse had that much courage. But to go on living we needed that one hero mouse. We would all watch her and cheer her on and feel inspired by what she did."

"That's interesting," I told Tommy. "Did you know, Tommy, that we Christians need the same kind of heroes? People who show us how to live. People who show us how not to be afraid of our enemies. People like Moses who ran up Pharaoh's clock, like Samson who ran up the Philistines' clock, and like Daniel who ran up Belshazzar's clock."

"Well," Tommy said as he waved good-bye with his tail, "I'm glad to hear that you've got some heroes too."

Being Gray

One evening when I stepped into the church, Tommy Tittlemouse was waiting for me. He was carrying something in his mouth—a piece of paper.

"What's that piece of paper, Tommy?"

"It's a poem I wrote. Do you know who Kermit the Frog is, Pastor?"

"Yes, I do," I told him. "He's one of my favorite TV characters."

"I'm glad to hear that," Tommy said, "for this poem was inspired by a song Kermit sings."

"Why don't you read it to me?" I asked.

"I'm going to," Tommy said. And this is the poem he read:

It's not easy being gray.
It's not easy being gray all day,
When I think it would be so much nicer
Being red or yellow, black or white,
Or something even more colorful in our sight.
It's not easy being gray.
It seems you blend in with so many things—
Things neither red or yellow, black or white,
But somewhere in between.
People pass you by 'cause they simply don't see you
Like they do flowers in the field
Or stars in the sky.
But gray is a color you find in the Bible.
The beauty of old people, the Bible says,

Is their gray hair.
And gray can be as wide as the ocean
Or as high as the sky,
Giving you a feeling of what God is like.
I am gray and I'm glad I am,
'Cause gray is beautiful.
Gray is what God made me.
Gray is what I always want to be.

When Tommy was finished reading, he gave the poem to me. Then, without saying a word, he disappeared into the darkness. Every once in a while I read the poem, and I'm amazed how a gray mouse like Tommy could write such a colorful poem.

Three-Legged Chickens

Once there was a salesman who went from farm to farm selling chicken feed. One day, as he drove away from a farm, he noticed that a chicken was running alongside his car. Though the car was moving at a pretty good speed, the chicken was keeping up. *How strange!* the salesman thought. *How very strange!* He stepped on the gas till he was going seventy miles an hour. Still the chicken kept up with the car.

What's going on here? the salesman wondered. He slowed down to take a good look at the chicken. What he saw was something he'd never seen before. The chicken had not two legs but three legs.

"This is crazy," the salesman mumbled to himself. "I must get to the bottom of this." So he turned his car around and went back to the farm he had left a couple of minutes ago. There he talked to the farmer. "Did you know that one of your chickens has three legs?" the salesman asked.

"Yes, I do," the farmer said.

"Do you have more of these chickens?" the salesman asked.

"Oh, yes, lots of them," the farmer said.

Then the salesman asked, "Where did you get those three-legged chickens?"

"I raised them myself," the farmer said. "We did some operating and experimenting and finally produced some three-legged chickens. You see, there are three of us—myself, my wife, and my son. We all like to eat chicken legs. Now with two-legged chickens we have to kill two chickens for each of us to have a chicken leg. But with three-legged chickens we only have to kill one chicken for each of us to have a chicken leg. And that's a lot cheaper. So I decided to go with three-legged chickens."

"That's amazing," the salesman said. "Tell me something, how do three-legged chickens taste?"

"I have no idea," the farmer said. "You see, those three-legged chickens are so fast, I've never been able to catch one."

Which goes to show that everything God made is good the way it is, and when we try to make better what God has made good, things get away from us like those three-legged chickens got away from the farmer.

Mister Know-It-All

Once upon a time, there was a poor but generous farmer. Each evening, he poured some milk in a dish and put it on a big stone. The next morning the dish was always empty. He was so poor that he could hardly spare the milk. But this dish of milk was his daily gift to God.

One evening, just as the farmer was putting his dish of milk on the stone, along came Mister Know-It-All. "What are you doing?" he asked the farmer.

The farmer told him, "I'm giving this milk to God. I do this every day. God always drinks the milk. Every morning the dish is empty."

"Don't be stupid," Mister Know-It-All said. "God doesn't drink your milk. An animal does. I'll tell you what. Why don't you and I hide behind that big tree over there, watch the dish of milk, and see what happens? The moon is out, so we should have no problem seeing who drinks the milk."

And that's what they did. They hid behind the tree and watched the dish. After an hour, a fox jumped on top of the stone, drank the milk, and disappeared.

"What did I tell you?" Mister Know-It-All said. "God doesn't drink your milk; animals do."

The farmer didn't say anything. He was disappointed. And very confused.

That night God spoke to Mister Know-It-All in a dream. "Know-It-All! What did you do to my good friend? Every day he did something beautiful for me. Even though I myself don't drink milk, I made a lot of animals that do. The way I see it, all the milk the farmer gives to animals he gives to me."

Colors

Ionce read a poem that went something like this:

Once Grandpa dropped his glasses in a pot of dye,
And when he put them on again, he saw a purple sky.

You understand that poem, don't you? What it means is that if you wear glasses that are red, everything looks red. And if you wear glasses that are yellow, everything looks yellow. And if you wear glasses that are purple, everything looks purple. Your pants look purple. Your dress looks purple. Your mom's hair looks purple. Your dog looks purple. Your toothpaste looks purple. Your milk looks purple. The sky looks purple. Everything looks purple.

Now wouldn't that be terrible if everything were one color? Wouldn't that be dull? Wouldn't that be awfully boring? So aren't you glad that God created colors? Aren't you glad that God created hundreds of different colors? Aren't you glad that your dress looks red and your pants gray and your mom's hair black and your dog brown and your milk white and the sky blue?

The Little Fir Tree

On the first Christmas, so an old story goes, all the animals in the world went to visit Jesus. Not just animals went, some of the trees did too.

Among the trees was a little fir tree. The tree could hardly walk, yet somehow it managed to keep up with the animals.

When the little fir tree arrived at the stable where Jesus was born, there were so many animals pushing and shoving that it had a hard time getting inside. And once inside, the little fir tree was pushed into a dark corner where no one could see it.

From where it was standing, the little fir tree could not see Jesus, and Jesus could not see the little fir tree. This made the little fir tree feel sad, for it so wanted to see baby Jesus smile.

Now in the stable there was an angel who was keeping an eye on things. Seeing the sad little fir tree in a dark corner, the angel called some stars to come down from the sky and sit on the tree's branches.

And so it happened. Stars came down from the sky and lit up the little fir tree. Suddenly the little fir tree was beautiful—more beautiful than all the animals in the stable. Everybody looked and was amazed. Then baby Jesus looked at the little fir tree and smiled. And that smile made the little fir tree happiest of all.

(Adapted from the December 21, 1979 issue of *The Banner*.)

A Bright Light

Ionce heard a beautiful story of two angels—an older angel and a younger angel. The older angel was showing the younger angel around the universe. When they came to our galaxy, the older angel pointed to a tiny planet and said, "You see that tiny planet over there in the far corner of the galaxy? I want you to watch it because it is the planet Jesus visited."

"You mean it is the planet Jesus visited on Christmas Day?"

"Exactly," the older angel said.

"But how?" the younger angel asked. "How did Jesus visit that tiny planet? Did he turn into one of those tiny creatures I see crawling all over that planet?"

"Yes, he did," the older angel said. "Now close your eyes for just a second, young angel, and we will go back in time."

The younger angel closed its eyes and immediately traveled back two thousand years to the time right before Jesus visited our planet.

"Now open your eyes and tell me what you see," the older angel said.

"What I see," the younger angel said, "are a few lights."

"Those," the older angel explained, "are the people who are looking forward to the coming of Jesus. There are only a few of them. All the others are not looking forward to the coming of Jesus. They make the planet look so terribly dark."

Right after the older angel had said that, a very bright light appeared on the planet. The light was so bright that the two angels had to cover their eyes.

"I know what that light is," the younger angel said. "That's Jesus' visit, isn't it?"

"Exactly," the older angel said. "But now watch! Watch how quickly that bright light will go out again. People will seek to put it out as fast as they can, for they love the darkness rather than the light."

And sure enough. It didn't take long, and the bright light went out.

"Is that the end of the bright light?" the younger angel asked.

"No, it isn't," the older angel answered. "Now let's go forward in time. Let's go forward to the year 2000, and you will see what happened to that bright light."

After the two angels arrived in the year 2000, the older angel said, "What do you see?"

"What I see," the younger angel said, "is millions and millions of tiny lights all over the planet."

"Those tiny lights," the older angel said, "are Christians who are bringing Jesus' bright light to all the dark places, until someday this planet will be as bright as Jesus himself."

Kissing in Church

My mother's family were kissers. My father's family were handshakers. When I visited my father's family, family members would shake my hand and say, "How are you, Johnny? It's good to see you." But when I visited my mother's family, family members would hug and kiss me. I especially remember one aunt. I called her Aunt Wetkiss. She would kiss me on the cheeks and leave both of them slightly wet.

I thought of that aunt last week. When I was reading the Bible, I came across these words: "Greet one another with a holy kiss."

Nineteen hundred years ago, when Christians in the city of Rome came together to worship God, they greeted one another with a holy kiss. They would say, "Good to see you, brother Antonias!" (kiss, kiss) and, "So glad to see you, sister Sylvia!" (kiss, kiss).

That was nineteen hundred years ago. But Christians don't do that much anymore. When we go to church on Sunday, we don't greet everyone with a holy kiss. Why not?

Maybe this is why. Maybe there were too many Christians like my aunt. Maybe there were too many Christian wetkissers, so that people began to say, "I don't care much for holy kisses. I don't like having all these people wet my cheeks with their kisses."

What do you think? What about those holy kisses in church? Should we forget about them? Or should we start giving them again?

Enjoying Life

I once heard a story of a poor fisherman. One day this fisherman was sitting on the dock next to his boat, looking out across the sea, watching the seagulls overhead, breathing the fresh air, and enjoying every minute of it.

After a while a rich man came along, sat down next to the fisherman, and asked him, "Why aren't you out there fishing?"

"I'm not fishing out there," the fisherman said, "because I've caught enough fish for the day."

"Why don't you catch some more?" the rich man asked.

And the fisherman answered, "What would I do with the fish?"

"You would earn more money," the rich man said. "And with that more money you could buy a motor for your boat and go into deeper waters and catch even more fish and make even more money. Pretty soon you would make enough money to own three boats instead of one. With those three boats you would make so much money that after a while you could own ten boats. Then, after a while, you would make so much money that you would be as rich as I am."

"What would I do then?" the fisherman asked.

"Then you would really enjoy life," the rich man said.

"What do you think I am doing right now?" the fisherman asked. "I am enjoying life without all that money."

That's a story to think about!

(Adapted from Anthony de Mello, *The Song of the Bird* [New York: Image Books, 1984], 132f.)

Sitting Still in Church

Recently I sat behind a mother and her four-year-old daughter in church. The little girl didn't sit still for a minute. All through the service she wiggled and squirmed and talked to her doll. She didn't bother me at all. It was her mother who got on my nerves. All she did was say to the girl, "Sit still! Be quiet! Sit still! Be quiet! Sit still! Be quiet!"

I thought, *Poor girl. She can't help it that she is wiggly and squirmy. That's the way God made her. Many children her age are that way. It's hard for children to sit still and be quiet for a whole hour.*

That little girl reminded me of a boy named Takashi. Many years ago, when I was a missionary in Japan, there was a wiggly and squirmy boy in our small church. His name was Takashi. One Sunday Takashi came to church with a wind-up car that made a lot of racket. As I was trying to preach in Japanese, Takashi suddenly decided that it was time for him to play with his toy car. His toy was louder than my voice, and I remember thinking, *Why doesn't Takashi's mother grab that car away from him and throw it out of the window?* But she didn't. She let him go on playing with it.

But that was not the worst thing that happened. One day Takashi fell off his father's motorbike and broke his leg. The leg was put in a cast and Takashi had to stay home from church. For a while things were very quiet in church. But not for very long. After a few weeks Takashi was back in church again, hopping on one leg. Thump, thump, thump! Every time Takashi thumped, which was every minute, the building shook as though there were an earthquake.

Last month, as I watched that little girl in front of me, I thought of Takashi. I thought, *Children are the same the world over. They're wiggly and squirmy at home and in church. And that's okay because that's the way God made them.*

Maybe grown-ups who are bothered by wiggly and squirmy children in church should say this prayer, "Dear God, thank you for all the wiggly and squirmy children here in church. Thank you for all the little children who can't sit still for a minute because they are children. Bless each one of them, even those who bring noisy toys to church. Amen."

Spite

About two hundred years ago something strange happened in Russia. The ruler of Russia at that time was a woman by the name of Elizabeth, and Elizabeth did the strangest things.

One day she told all the women in her palace to shave off their hair and start wearing wigs. The women moaned and groaned, but there was nothing they could do about it. They all had their hair shaved off, and they started to wear wigs.

Why did Elizabeth do this? She did it out of spite. Elizabeth, you see, was always fussing with her hair. One time she dyed her hair black. But then, a couple of days later when she looked in the mirror, she decided that she didn't like her hair black. She tried to wash the black dye out of her hair, but it wouldn't come out. So she had her hair shaved off and wore a wig. Then, because Elizabeth couldn't stand the idea that she had no hair while other women in the palace did, she made them shave off their hair and wear wigs. She did it out of spite.

Once when I was a young boy, my brother and I each had a balloon. But suddenly my balloon popped. Because I couldn't stand the idea that my brother had a balloon and I didn't, I popped his balloon. Out of spite.

The Bible says we must do things out of love, not out of spite. What's the difference? Well, one difference is that if you do things out of love, you won't pop someone else's balloon. Maybe you can think of another difference.

What Is God Like?

What is God like? If you want to know, listen to this story.

Once upon a time there was a little boy. Let's call him Johnny. Johnny was always coming home late from playing outside.

One day his mom and dad had had enough of it. They said, "Listen, Johnny! You never come home in time for supper. Your supper is always getting cold. We always have to warm it up for you. This has got to stop. Next time you come home late, we'll give you bread and water. That's all. No butter, no peanut butter, no jam. Just plain bread and water."

Well, the next day Johnny came home late for supper again. He walked into the house and sat down at the supper table. His mom and dad, who had plates with meat and potatoes and vegetables in front of them, didn't say a thing. They quietly gave Johnny a plate with some bread and a glass of water.

Johnny was crushed. He never thought his mom and dad would do such a thing. How could they? But he was wrong.

Johnny's father waited for the lesson to sink in. Then, silently, he took his own plate full of meat and potatoes and vegetables, and put it in front of Johnny. Then he took Johnny's plate and put it in front of himself.

Johnny is now a man. Not too long ago Johnny said, "Do you know what God is like? I've known it all my life. I've known it ever since that night when my father switched plates."

That's a true story. It really happened.

Hunger

More than fifty years ago, when I was a teenager, there was a terrible war in the country where I was living. There also was a terrible famine. When there's a famine, people have no food. Sometimes during a famine people die because they have no food. Our family, too, was hungry; so hungry we could have eaten an elephant.

Now it so happened that a cousin of mine had a cat she wanted to get rid of. "Johnny," she asked, "can you get rid of my cat?"

"No problem," I said.

I took the cat home, showed it to my family, and said, "Let's eat it."

They said, "Eat it? Eat a cat? No way!"

But my older brother agreed. He and I killed and ate the cat. We were that hungry.

So now you know my secret. I'm probably the only minister in the United States who ever ate a cat.

This is the way I look at it. Each day when we pray "Give us this day our *daily* bread," God answers our prayer by providing food for us. But fifty years ago God said, "Sorry, but I'm out of bread right now. I'll give you a cat instead, for I don't want you to die."

I remember another story—another true story—of what happened in my hometown during the famine more than fifty years ago.

I had a good friend whose name was Peter. In Peter's family there were five children, five hungry children.

One day Peter's father told his family, "Sorry, but we're out of food. There's nothing more for us to eat."

Peter's mother got angry—angry at God. She said, "How can God do that to us? How can God let us starve to death? Didn't Jesus teach us to pray for our daily bread? Well, we've done that. We have prayed for our daily bread. So where is it?" Peter's mother got so angry that she shook her fist at God and said, "I hate you, God!"

Right after Peter's mother had said that, the doorbell rang. Peter's father opened the door. It was the baker. In his hand he held a loaf of bread. He said, "I had an extra loaf of bread. I thought your family might need it." Then he gave Peter's father the loaf of bread and left.

Peter's father went back to the living room, put the loaf of bread on the table, and said, "Here is our daily bread."

Then Peter's mother broke down and cried until she had used up all her tears. Then she said, "Forgive me, God. Thank you for giving us our daily bread."

Next time you pray, "Give us this day our daily bread," think of these stories.

Cheating God

Once there lived a woman who'd never been sick a day in her whole life. Then, one day, it happened. She got sick. And did she get sick. She got so sick she thought she was going to die. So she prayed, "Please, God, make me better. If you make me better, I will sell my house and give all the money from the sale of the house to the poor."

God answered her prayer. The sick woman got better. But when she got better, she had second thoughts about her promise to God. She thought, *Sell my house and give all the money to the poor? My home is worth a lot of money, at least one hundred thousand dollars. Whatever made me promise God to give all this money to the poor?*

So the woman made a plan. She decided to sell her house and her cat together. No one could buy one without buying the other. She decided to sell her house for ten dollars and her cat for one hundred thousand dollars. She put the following ad in the newspaper:

FOR SALE: ONE HOUSE FOR $10 AND ONE CAT FOR $100,000. WILL NOT SELL SEPARATELY. MUST BUY BOTH HOUSE AND CAT.

Of course, everybody wanted to buy the house for ten dollars without buying the cat for one hundred thousand dollars. But the woman said, "No, you can't buy one without the other. You can't buy the house without buying the cat."

Well, finally the woman found a buyer. She got ten dol-

(Adapted from Edward Hays, *In Pursuit of the Great White Rabbit* [Leavenworth, Kan.: Forest of Peace, 1990].)

lars for the house and one hundred thousand dollars for the cat. Then she gave the ten dollars she got from the sale of the house to the poor, and she kept the one hundred thousand dollars she got from the sale of the cat for herself.

Can you explain to your mom or dad why that isn't fair, why that's cheating God?

Dog Story

The city of Tokyo is one of the biggest cities in the world. It has many train stations. One of Tokyo's busiest stations is Shibuya. And right outside of Shibuya station there is a statue of a dog—a dog called Hachiko.

Hachiko belonged to a man named Mr. Ueno. Each morning, no matter what the weather, Hachiko walked Mr. Ueno to the Shibuya station, where Mr. Ueno caught the train. Hachiko always waited for Mr. Ueno to disappear into the station, then he turned around and went home. At the end of the day Hachiko returned to the station to pick up his master for the walk home.

One spring morning Hachiko walked his master to the station as usual. Mr. Ueno said, "See you this afternoon, my friend!" and left to catch his train. As usual, Hachiko watched his master disappear before going home.

That afternoon Hachiko returned to the station at the usual hour. He waited and waited and waited. But his master did not show up. That afternoon Mr. Ueno had suddenly died, but of course, Hachiko didn't know that. Hachiko waited several hours. Then he walked home alone.

But the next day Hachiko went to the station again to wait for his master to come. He went again and again, day after day, year in year out.

One morning, almost ten years after his master had died, Hachiko went to Shibuya station as usual. By this time he was an old dog, and making the trip to the station was harder and harder for him. He waited at the usual place. All of a sudden he fell over and died.

The people of Tokyo were so touched by Hachiko's faithfulness that they made a statue in his memory. When I lived in Japan, I passed by the statue many times. Each time I saw the statue I thought, *If this dog, whom God created, was so utterly faithful, can you imagine how faithful God must be—God who created this dog?*

Waiting for the Benediction

Have you ever heard of Albert Schweitzer? If you haven't, listen to this story.

Albert Schweitzer was a famous organist. He was also a medical doctor. And he was a missionary to Africa.

When Albert Schweitzer was a young boy, he lived in a small village in Germany, where his dad was a minister. Every Sunday Albert went to church and listened to his dad's sermons. But young Albert had a problem. Even though he listened to his dad's sermons, there was much in the sermons he didn't understand.

Still, Albert loved to go to church. He loved to sing hymns and hear the organ play. But what do you think little Albert loved the most about church? What he loved the most was the benediction, the blessing, at the end of the service. He loved the moment when his dad raised his hands and said:

The Lord bless you and keep you;
the Lord make his face to shine upon you,
*   and be gracious to you;*
the Lord lift up his countenance upon you,
*   and give you peace.*

When his dad spoke those words, young Albert felt warm inside.

Do you know why? Do you know what happens when a minister says the benediction? What happens is that God blesses you. God lays his hand on your head and says to you, "Pretty soon when you leave church and go home, I'm going with you. And all week long I'll be watching over you."

Next Sunday when you go to church and hear the benediction, I hope you, too, will feel warm inside just as Albert Schweitzer did when he was your age.

The Hot Stone

People living in the middle of Africa have a game. They take a stone and put it in the fire until it is very hot. Then a group of men form a circle, and one of them takes the stone out of the fire. Because the stone is very hot, he can't hold it in his hands. So what does he do? He quickly throws it to the next man, who then quickly throws it to the next man, and so on, around the circle.

Any man who doesn't throw the stone quickly, burns his hands. So the trick of the game is to catch and throw the stone as fast as possible.

Evil is like that hot stone. Evil burns, so people quickly pass it on to the next person. Let me give you two examples.

When I was a little boy, I could just reach the sugar bowl on top of the tea cabinet in our living room. I would stand on tiptoe, wet my finger, dip it in the sugar bowl, and lick it off.

But of course, I would always leave behind a trail of sugar on the tea cabinet. And of course, my mother would see the sugar and ask, "Who's been eating sugar?"

Then I would point my sticky sugary finger at my brother and say, "Martin did it." You see, I threw the hot stone to my brother.

Adam and Eve did the same thing. When God asked Adam, "Why did you eat from the tree of which I told you not to eat?" Adam answered, "Eve made me do it." Quickly Adam threw the hot stone to Eve.

And what did Eve do? When God asked her why she ate from the tree of which God told her not to eat, Eve said, "I ate because the snake deceived me." Quickly Eve threw the hot stone to the snake.

You children sometimes do the same thing, don't you? You do something bad and get caught. And what do you do? You blame your brother or sister or friend. Quickly you throw the hot stone to them.

What we all should do is drop the hot stone at our own feet and not throw it to someone else. What we should do is take the blame for the bad thing we did, say we're sorry we did it, and ask God to forgive us.

Pussycat, Pusscat

Last summer we traveled to the Rocky Mountains. One day we took a walk to a point where we had a most beautiful view: blue skies, snow-covered mountains, and a green valley. God could not have made anything more beautiful than that.

While we were standing there, I noticed two boys, each with a new camera. I thought, *Good for them! They're going to take pictures of this grand scene.* But I was wrong. They were taking pictures of some silly chipmunks playing hide-and-seek among the rocks. They were totally blind to the huge mountains and spent their time looking at animals they probably had in their backyard.

The boys reminded me of this nursery rhyme:

Pussycat, pussycat: Where have you been?
I've been to London, to visit the queen.
Pussycat, pussy at: What did you do there?
I frightened a little mouse under her chair.

Let's do some pretending. Pretend that tomorrow your cat receives a letter from the queen of England. The letter says, "Dear Pussycat, I, Queen of England, invite you to come and visit me at my palace in London."

The next day you take your cat to the airport. Before she boards the plane, you tell her, "When you sit on the queen's lap, don't put out your sharp claws. Just purr! That's all you have to do. Purr!"

When your cat arrives in London, a limousine is waiting to drive her to the palace. Here one of the queen's servants tells her, "Follow me!" They come to the queen's room; the servant knocks.

From inside the room the queen calls, "Come in!" As the door opens, your cat sees a little mouse under the queen's chair. She does not look at the queen. Instead she begins chasing the mouse.

A couple of days later your cat returns home. At the airport you ask her, "How was the queen?"

And your cat answers, "I don't know. I never sat on her lap. Instead I frightened a little mouse under her chair."

"What?" you say. "You flew all the way to London to do what you do every day here at home?"

That's sad, isn't it? It's sad when we take pictures of silly chipmunks instead of beautiful mountains. It's sad when we chase a little mouse instead of sitting on the queen's lap. It's sad when we pay attention to small things and fail to see big things.

I hope you're not like that pussycat. When the queen of England invites you to her palace, I hope you'll sit on her lap and talk to her awhile. Forget all about that silly little mouse under her chair.

A Safe Path

About 250 years ago, 900 Waldensians—men, women, and children—decided to go back to Italy—their home country.

"Who in the world are the Waldensians?" you ask. "Never heard of them."

The Waldensians are Christians who many centuries ago left the Roman Catholic Church. "Too many things are wrong with the Roman Catholic Church," they said. So they left it.

"You are leaving our church? Why not leave our country too?" many people said, and they chased the Waldensians out of Italy.

After living in another country for a while, 900 Waldensians decided to go back to Italy. When they came to the Italian border, they found more than 2000 soldiers blocking their way. "We won't let you in," the soldiers said. "Go back where you came from."

"Now what?" the Waldensians asked their leader. "What shall we do? What can we do?"

The leader answered, "We can pray and we will pray."

Now as they were praying, one of the Waldensians touched the leader on his shoulder and said, "Sir, I was once a shepherd in this area. I know this area very well. I know a mountain path that leads around the soldiers into Italy. The path is steep and dangerous. But it leads home."

(Adapted from Charles L. Wallis, editor, *Treasury of Story Sermons for Children* [New York: Harper, 1957], 190–193.)

The Waldensians waited till it was dark. Then their leader said to the shepherd, "Lead us to your path."

Holding hands so that no one would get separated, the Waldensians slowly followed the shepherd. They followed him for many hours. Finally, when the sun rose above the horizon, they were safely in Italy—their home country.

They stopped and formed a circle around their leader. The leader said, "Before we lie down and rest, let us thank God for using our shepherd friend to lead us down a safe path." And then the leader recited a psalm that speaks of God the Shepherd leading his people down a safe path:

The Lord is my shepherd, I shall not want.
He makes me lie down in green pastures;
He leads me beside still waters;
He restores my soul.
He leads me in right paths . . .

Pray that someday God will use you to lead people down a safe path.

Humpty Dumpty

Humpty Dumpty sat on a wall,
Humpty Dumpty had a great fall.
All the king's horses
And all the king's men
Couldn't put Humpty together again.

That may sound like a silly rhyme, but it isn't. It isn't as silly as it sounds. It asks this very important question: If all the king's horses and all the king's men couldn't put Humpty Dumpty together again, who could? Was there anyone, anyone at all, who could pick up the broken pieces and put Humpty Dumpty together again?

Do you remember the story in the Bible of the boy who would foam at the mouth, grind his teeth, and throw himself into the fire or into the water? This poor boy was so miserable that he wanted to destroy himself. He was a Humpty-Dumpty boy. No doctor could put him back together again.

So the boy's father said, "If the doctors can't make my son better, maybe Jesus can." He traveled to the place where Jesus was supposed to be. But Jesus wasn't there.

The disciples told the father, "Sorry, but Jesus is up on the mountain."

Then the father asked Jesus' disciples, "Can you please put my Humpty-Dumpty son back together again?" They tried, but they couldn't help him.

If only Jesus would come back, the father thought. And suddenly, there he was.

"What's going on?" Jesus asked. When the father told

him, Jesus made the boy whole. Jesus put the Humpty-Dumpty boy back together again.

So this nursery rhyme isn't as silly as it sounds. What it says is true. All the king's horses and all the king's men couldn't put Humpty Dumpty together again. It took the king himself to do that. It took King Jesus himself.

What Would You Have Said?

On December 6, 1944, guess what I was doing? With my older brother, Martin, I was hiding from enemy soldiers. We were hiding under the floor.

It was toward the end of World War II. The enemy badly needed people to keep their factories going. So they arrested boys my age and older to get workers.

On December 6, 1944, enemy soldiers blocked off our entire city and began a house-to-house search for people old enough to work for them. At around eleven o'clock in the morning they began searching the houses in our street.

Some months earlier my dad had made an opening in the kitchen floor. When the search began, my brother and I slipped through this hole and disappeared under the floor. My dad closed the hole and covered it with a rug. Then he put the kitchen table and a chair on the rug.

My brother and I quickly crawled toward the front hall. You see, the front hall had a stone floor, and hiding beneath a stone floor was the safest. Sometimes enemy soldiers would shoot through a floor if they thought people might be hiding below it.

Soon we heard a knock at the door. My older sister opened the door.

"Where is your father?" a soldier asked, and he stepped inside the door and stood right above our hiding place. When my dad came, the soldier asked, "Do you have sons?"

My dad said, "No, I don't."

"Is that the truth?" the soldier asked.

"Feel free to search the house," my dad answered.

But the soldier didn't search. He saluted and left.

My question is: When the enemy soldier asked my dad, "Do you have sons?" should he have answered, "Yes, I do"? And if the soldier had then asked, "Where are they?" should my dad have answered, "They're hiding right below where you are standing"?

If you had been my dad, what would you have said?

A Scary Story

This story may be a little bit scary. If you'd rather not listen to it, just stick your fingers in your ears.

Once, long ago and far away, a man was traveling through a wilderness. Suddenly he spotted a lion. The lion came toward him. The man thought, *I'm in trouble. This lion wants to kill me.*

So the man started to run. He ran and ran until he spotted a well. To escape the lion, he climbed over the side of the well. The well, he found, was very deep, but it was also dry. *Am I lucky,* the traveler told himself. *There's no water in the well.* But then, as he looked down, he saw that the bottom of the well was crawling with poisonous snakes.

The poor man didn't dare climb out of the well for fear that the lion would kill him. But neither did he dare jump to the bottom of the well for fear that the snakes would kill him. So with both hands he grabbed onto a branch that was growing out of the side of the well.

There he was between the lion and the snakes holding on for dear life to the branch. After a while his hands grew tired, and he knew that he couldn't hold on much longer.

Then, horror of horrors, he spotted a mouse. The mouse was nibbling away at the same branch he was holding onto. *Oh no,* the man thought, *soon the branch will be nibbled through and I will drop down to the bottom of the well and land in the middle of all the snakes. Who can save me?*

Good question. Who can save the man? He can't save himself. Someone must kill the lion, reach down into the well, and grab hold of the poor man to save him.

We are in the same position as that traveler. We cannot save ourselves. Someone from the outside must reach down into our lives, grab hold of us, and save us. And, of course, you know who that someone is. I don't have to tell you that.

What Killed the Dog?

There once was a farmer who went on vacation for a couple of weeks. When he returned home, his neighbor picked him up at the train station.

"What's new?" the farmer asked. "Did anything important happen while I was gone?"

"Not really," the neighbor answered.

"Oh, come on," the farmer said. "Something must have happened while I was gone."

"Not really," the neighbor answered. "Oh, one thing did happen. Your dog died."

"My dog died? How did that happen?"

"He ate some burnt horse meat. That's what killed your dog."

"He ate some burnt horse meat? Whose horse burned to death?"

"Your horse did!" the neighbor answered. "And your dog ate some of that burnt horse meat. That's what killed your dog."

"My horse burned to death? How did that happen?"

"Your horse burned to death because your barn burned down. Your horse was in the barn. Then your dog ate some of that burnt horse meat. That's what killed your dog."

"My barn burned down!" the farmer exclaimed. "How did that happen?"

"The way I figure it is that sparks must have fallen on top of the barn roof. The sparks set off the fire that burned your barn and your horse. Then your dog ate some of that burnt horse meat. And that's what killed your dog."

"Sparks fell on top of the barn roof? Where did those sparks come from?" yelled the farmer.

"From your house," the neighbor said. "You see, your house was on fire. Sparks from your burning house set your barn on fire and burned your horse. Then the dog ate some of that burnt horse meat. And that's what killed your dog."

Do you think that by that time the farmer still wanted to talk about what happened to his dog? I don't think so. He had more important things to talk about. But his neighbor kept explaining what killed the dog.

You'd be surprised how many people are like the farmer's neighbor. They're afraid to talk about the important things in life. All they talk about are the unimportant things. Each time someone talks about serious things, they change the subject.

Have you ever met people like that? If you haven't, you will. When you do, think of the story I just told you.

Jesus, Pilot Me

A couple of years ago I flew in a twin-engine plane. I'll be honest; I don't like small planes. When we started down the runway, the plane swerved as though it were drunk. I thought, *What if this plane is drunk? What if it runs on wine? What if it has had too much wine?* But once we were in the air, the plane sobered up and flew straight.

After a while I thought, "What if one of the two propellers comes off? Would the pilot be able to land the plane?" But then I remembered reading somewhere that, yes, good pilots can land a plane even if it has only one propeller, and I felt a lot better.

After a while I thought, *What if one of the wings breaks off? Would the pilot be able to land the plane?* And I remembered reading somewhere that, no, that's not possible. If a wing breaks off a plane, the plane goes spiraling down. The more I thought about the wing, the more worried I got.

After a while I thought, *What if something happens to the pilot? What if the pilot turns around and says to me, 'I don't feel so good. I think I'm going to pass out.' Then what? Then I would have to land the plane. Then I would have to radio ground control and say, 'Ground control, ground control! Can you hear me?' Ground control would say, 'Yes, we can hear you. What's the problem?' And then I would say, 'The pilot just passed out and I'm the only passenger on this twin-engine plane. What do I do?' And then ground control would say, 'Sir, do you have a pilot license?' And I would say, 'No, I don't. All I have is a preaching license.' And then ground* control would say, 'That's not going to help you any, sir.' And I would say, 'I know.'

As I was flying in that small plane I thought, *My life is just like this small plane. I'm glad I'm not the pilot. I'm glad Jesus is the pilot of my life. I'm glad I can pray, 'Jesus, Savior, pilot me.'*

How Long Is God's Nose?

How long is your nose? Not very long, is it? If you stick out your tongue, you can't even touch your nose. And if you look at it with both eyes, you can't even see it.

But what if your nose were as long as your hand, or worse, as long as your arm? What then?

Then you would have to move slowly. For if you didn't, people would constantly bump into your nose and bend it.

Then you would be saying things like, "Hey! Will you please watch where you are going? You just bent my nose!"

And then others would be saying, "Oh, I'm sorry. Here, let me help you straighten it back into shape."

If your nose were as long as your arm, you would also have to control your anger. You would have to be slow to anger. For if you didn't control your anger, you might get into some horrible fights. Someone might grab your nose and tie a knot in it. Or someone might swing you around by the nose a couple of times and then let you go flying through the air like they do in cartoons sometimes.

When you are long of nose, you mustn't get angry easily.

You know, God doesn't get angry easily. That's what the Bible says. In the original language in which the Bible was written, it says that God is "long of nose." That doesn't mean that God has a nose like yours and mine and that God's nose is very long. What it means is that God does not become angry easily and that, when God does become angry, he does not stay angry for very long. God is slow to anger, and that's why we who are God's children must be slow to anger too. We must be "long of nose."

Ora et Labora

I had eight uncles. I *had* eight uncles, but they're all dead now. All eight of them were Christians. Some talked little about their faith; others talked about their faith a lot. The one who talked about it the most was my Uncle Biem.

Uncle Biem had a dairy store, where he sold milk and cheese and butter and eggs. He gave that store a strange name. He called it *Ora et Labora*.

The words are Latin and they mean "pray and work." An odd name for a dairy store, don't you think? I don't think there's ever been a dairy store by that name before or since. But that's what Uncle Biem called his store. For, he said, to receive God's blessing we must both pray and work. We must pray as though everything depends on God, and we must work as though everything depends on us.

That's true, isn't it? You can't very well ask God to bless your work when you're lazy. You can't very well ask God to bless your homework when you're playing or watching TV instead of studying.

Have you ever heard of Martin Luther? Martin Luther, who lived about five hundred years ago, worked hard to make things better in the church. He worked hard on the sermons he preached.

Once when Martin Luther was working on a sermon he had to preach the next Sunday, one of his friends said, "Martin, you're spending way too much time on that sermon. There are so many other things you should be doing. Why don't you ask God to do the preaching for you? Why not ask

God to speak to you while you're preaching next Sunday? That will save you a lot of time."

"Okay," Martin Luther said. "That's what I'll do."

A few days after Martin had preached his sermon, the friend came to see him. "Well, Martin, did God speak to you during the sermon?"

"Yes, he did," Martin Luther said. "He certainly did."

"Well, what did God say?" his friend asked.

Luther answered, "God told me I'd been lazy!"

We must pray and work. We must work as if everything depends on us and pray as if everything depends on God. *Ora et labora.*

How to Make Gold

Once, long ago and far away, there was an old woman. Every day this old woman sat in front of an old pot and stirred what was in it. And what was in the pot was just plain old dirt and water.

After hours of stirring, the old woman would reach into the pot and pull out a big lump of gold. And each time she pulled out a lump of gold, the people standing around her got very excited. But not the old woman. The lumps of gold didn't excite her in the least.

One day a young woman who was greedy for gold asked the old woman, "Will you please show me how you do your trick?"

"It's very simple," the old woman said. "Take an old pot, fill it with plain old dirt and water, and stir it. After a while a lump of gold appears. Just reach down and lift it out."

So that's what the greedy young woman did. She took an old pot, filled it with dirt and water, and began stirring. She stirred and stirred and stirred, but no lump of gold appeared.

After a couple of days she went back to the old woman and said, "I did what you told me, but the trick doesn't work."

"Tell me step by step what you did," the old woman said.

The greedy young woman told the old woman exactly what she did.

When she finished, the old woman said, "The reason it didn't work is because I forgot to tell you one important thing. I forgot to tell you that while you are stirring you must never think about the gold."

What the old woman was telling that greedy young woman was this: Don't set your heart on gold! Don't set your heart on money! Set your heart on something higher, something more important! When you do, money somehow will always be there when you need it.

That sounds like the kind of thing Jesus might have said, don't you think?

The Other Wise Man

Most of you know the story of the wise men from the East who came to worship baby Jesus, the newborn king of the Jews. But have you ever heard the story of the other wise man? Have you ever heard the story of the wise man who told the others, "You just go on ahead. I'll catch up with you later"? Even though this story is not in the Bible and didn't really happen, I think you'll enjoy listening to it.

After the other wise man told his friends to go ahead, he sold everything he had. With the money, he bought three precious stones to give to Jesus. As he was hurrying to catch up with the others, he saw a man who had been badly beaten lying by the side of the road. He took the man to an inn and told the innkeeper, "Take care of this poor man. Here is a precious stone to pay for his care." Then the wise man continued on his journey.

After several days he arrived in Bethlehem. The villagers told him about a mysterious baby who had been born in a stable. Angels, they said, had sung on the night when this baby was born.

The other wise man stayed that night in the home of a young couple with a baby. In the middle of the night a loud knock woke them up. A neighbor shouted, "The soldiers of King Herod are killing all the young children!"

Quickly the other wise man jumped out of bed, and rushed to the door. As soon as he saw a soldier with a sword in his hand coming to the house, the other wise man showed

---

(Adapted from the well-known story by Henry Van Dyke.)

the soldier a precious stone. "You can have it," he said, "if you don't enter this house."

The soldier took the precious stone and walked on by.

Now the other wise man had only one precious stone left. *At least I have one precious stone left to give to the newborn king of the Jews,* he thought.

But no matter how hard he tried to find this king, he never did. Finally he gave up looking for the king and went back to his own country.

Thirty years went by. One day he heard that the king of the Jews was living in Palestine and was going around the country preaching and healing. Quickly he traveled to Palestine, to Jerusalem. There he was told that the person he was looking for was on his way to Golgotha to be crucified.

As he hurried to Golgotha, he passed by a slave market. A young slave girl begged him, "Please, sir, buy my freedom and set me free."

The other wise man sighed. "All right," he said, "I'll buy your freedom with my last precious stone."

And he did. He gave the slave owner his last precious stone and set the slave girl free.

Right then it turned dark, very dark. There was a big earthquake. Buildings began to crumble and fall. A stone wall fell on the other wise man.

As he lay dying, he asked God to forgive him for giving away his three precious stones instead of presenting them to Jesus, the king of the Jews. But then he heard a voice say, "Everything you did for others, you did for Jesus. Come and enter into the kingdom which Jesus has prepared for you."

And so, at last, the other wise man found Jesus.

Finger Prayer

Right before you go to bed, what do you do? You pray, right? You pray for other people. But how can you be sure that you won't forget anyone? Well, someone has thought of a way to help you remember whom to pray for.

Look at your hand, holding it as if you were going to suck your thumb. Which finger is closest to your mouth? Your thumb. So your thumb reminds you to pray for people who are closest to you—your brothers and your sisters and your friends.

The next finger is your index finger. The index finger is used to point and shake. "How many times have I told you to clean up your room?" your mom or dad will say, shaking an index finger at you. The index finger expresses authority. It reminds you to pray for people who are in authority over you—your mom and your dad and your teachers.

The next finger is the middle finger. It is the highest finger. It reminds you to pray for your president or prime minister—those who are the highest in the country.

The next finger is the ring finger, the weakest of the five fingers. It reminds you to pray for people who are weak or sick or poor or hungry.

Finally, there is the little finger. The little finger is you. It reminds you to pray for yourself.

Let's see if you remember what I just told you. Every night before you go to bed you should pray for

- the people closest to you,
- the people who have authority over you,

- the president or prime minister,
- people who are weak, sick, poor, or hungry,
- yourself.

I hope this will help you remember whom to pray for.

Seeing Pearls

Once upon a time, so a Dutch fairy tale goes, there was a man whose name was Chris. Chris saw things no one else saw. He saw God in places where no one else saw God. This made people feel uncomfortable, so they asked him to leave town and live somewhere else.

That's what Chris did. He moved to a place where no one else lived. Here he built a home and was happy.

Every morning he would open his bedroom window, look outside, and say, "Look at those beautiful pearls on the flowers and grass! How rich I am! I must be the richest man in the whole world!"

Late one evening there was a knock at the door. "Who is there?" Chris asked.

"It's me," a voice said. "I'm a traveler and I'm very tired and hungry."

Chris invited the traveler in. He looked at the traveler for a long time without saying a word. It had been many years since Chris had seen another human being, and he didn't know what to say.

Finally the traveler gave Chris a golden coin. "Here," he said, "maybe this will help. How about giving me some food?"

But Chris said, "Keep your money. I don't need it." He went to the cupboard and soon the traveler had all the food he could eat.

After the traveler had eaten, he asked, "Why don't you want my money?"

"Because," Chris said, "I don't need it. I'm rich. I'm the richest man in the world. I have millions and millions of pearls."

When the traveler heard this, he turned pale. "You have millions and millions of pearls?" he stuttered. "Where are they?"

"Outside," Chris said, "sprinkled all across my fields."

"That's hard to believe," the traveler said. "If you have whole fields full of pearls, you must indeed be rich."

"That's what I told you," Chris said. "I'm the richest man in the world."

"I must leave right away," said the traveler. "This is the greatest discovery I've ever made. I must tell the people in the town about it."

"Yes, why don't you? Tell them that I would like to share the pearls with them," Chris said.

The traveler ran to the town and called all the townspeople together. "If you want pearls, follow me," the traveler said. Hundreds of townspeople followed him to Chris's house. The traveler called, "Chris, we've come for pearls. Show us where they are."

"Just follow me," said Chris. He led the people to the grassy field behind his house. Right then the sun came up, shedding its light across the field and making dewdrops on the grass shine like pearls. "There!" Chris said. "Aren't they beautiful? Pearls as far as you can see. Millions of pearls!"

"Pearls? Pearls? We don't see any pearls," the people said.

"You don't see any pearls?" Chris said. "Look around you! Don't you see them shining on the grass?"

"Those aren't pearls! Those are only dewdrops!" the people shouted angrily. "Is this why we have come all the way out here?"

Then someone shouted, "Hang him! Hang him from that tree!" And that's what the people did. They hanged Chris because he saw treasures where no one else did.

Doesn't this story remind you of the way people treated Jesus? Jesus, too, was hung on a tree. He was crucified. Why?

Because he saw treasures where no one else did. He saw God where no one else did. He looked at a field full of everyday lilies and said, "Look at all these treasures! The clothes God made for these lilies are more beautiful than the beautiful clothes King Solomon wore. If God paid so much attention to these simple flowers, don't you think he'll pay even more attention to you? Therefore, don't worry, saying, 'What will we wear?'"

Jesus saw things no one else saw. He saw God where no one else did. That's why people got angry at Jesus and, in the end, hung him on a tree.

Seeing It All

Once, long ago and far away, a king invited seven blind men to his palace. He told them, "I'd like to show you my elephants." So the seven blind men went to the king's stable and began to feel the elephants. Each felt a different part. Then the king asked the blind men, "Tell me, what is an elephant like?"

The first blind man said, "An elephant is like a pillar." This man had felt an elephant's leg.

The second blind man said, "An elephant is like a broom." This man had felt an elephant's tail.

The third blind man said, "An elephant is like lumps of dirt." This man had felt an elephant's belly.

The fourth blind man said, "An elephant is like a wall." This man had felt an elephant's side.

The fifth blind man said, "An elephant is like a hill." This man had felt an elephant's back.

The sixth blind man said, "An elephant is like a napkin." This man had felt an elephant's ear.

The seventh blind man said, "An elephant is like a horn." This man had felt an elephant's tusk.

Then all the blind men began to quarrel. The first one said to the second, "You're wrong. An elephant is not like a broom. An elephant is like a pillar." And the third one said to the fourth one, "You're wrong. An elephant is not like a wall. An elephant is like lumps of dirt." And the fifth one said to the sixth one, "You're wrong. An elephant is not like a napkin. An elephant is like a hill." On and on they argued because they were blind and could not see the whole elephant.

People have argued the same way about God. What is God like? One said, "God is like a king." A second one said, "God is like a prophet." A third one said, "God is like a shepherd." A fourth one said, "God is like a judge." A fifth one said, "God is like a friend." A sixth one said, "God is like bread." A seventh one said, "God is like water." On and on they argued because they could not see all of God.

What is God like? On Christmas Day God said, "I'll tell you what I am like. I am like Jesus. If you want to know what I am like, look at Jesus."

Outsmarting a Robber

Once, long ago and far away, so an old Jewish story goes, there was a carpenter. And this carpenter was a wise man, as we will soon learn. One day after a hard day's work, he was hurrying home with his pay safely hidden in his pocket.

To get home, the carpenter had to pass through a wood. As he hurried through the wood, a robber suddenly jumped from behind a tree, pointed a gun at him, and said, "Your money. I want your money. If you don't give me your money, I'll shoot."

The carpenter, who was not stupid but wise, gave the robber his money. As he handed over the money, the carpenter said, "You know, my wife isn't going to believe this. She'll say to me, 'A robber stole the money from you? Hah! I know what you did with the money. You spent it.' That's what my wife will say when I get home," the carpenter told the robber. "So I'd like you to do something for me."

"Well, what do you want me to do for you?" the robber asked.

"What I want is this," the carpenter said. "Shoot a bullet through my hat. Then when I get home, I'll show the hat to my wife and say, 'When I ran away from the robber, he fired his gun at me and the bullet went right through my hat.' My wife will be impressed."

The robber thought this was very funny, so he took the carpenter's hat, threw it up in the air, and shot a bullet through it. When he handed the hat back, he asked, "Will that be all?"

"Well, if you really want to help me," the carpenter said, "you could also shoot a bullet through the sleeve of my coat. That will make things look good. My wife will be even more impressed."

"No problem!" the robber said, and he shot a bullet through the sleeve.

"One more request," the carpenter said. "To make things look even better, why don't you shoot a bullet through the other sleeve as well? My wife will be so impressed, she'll think I'm a hero."

"I can't," the robber said. "I'm out of bullets."

"You are?" the carpenter said, and with one good punch he knocked down the robber, took back his money, and went on his way singing.

In the Bible it says that a wise general can take a city defended by strong soldiers by outsmarting them (see Proverbs 21:22). Doesn't this saying sound like our story? A wise carpenter met a robber with a gun and outsmarted him.

Tomato Jo

Once upon a time there was a woman who loved tomatoes. She ate tomatoes for breakfast. She ate tomatoes for lunch. She ate tomatoes for dinner. And she ate tomatoes for snacks. All she ate was tomatoes—tomatoes so red and ripe that when she sank her teeth in them juice squirted in all directions. In fact, there was dried tomato juice on all of her shirts and jeans. Some people said that the woman also bathed in tomato juice, but we're not sure about that. Maybe she did, and maybe she didn't. But it will come as no surprise that everybody called her Tomato Jo.

Of course, buying so many tomatoes costs a lot of money. So one day Tomato Jo decided to grow her own tomatoes. She went to the store and asked for tomato seeds.

"I don't have tomato seeds," the store owner said, "but I do have carrot seeds."

Tomato Jo bought the carrot seeds, went home, and planted them in her garden. But instead of pouring water on the carrot seeds, she poured tomato juice on them. *This way,* she thought, *I will grow tomatoes instead of carrots.*

She was wrong. For as the plants grew bigger and bigger, they grew carrots and not tomatoes.

So Tomato Jo went back to the store. She said, "I don't want carrots. I want tomatoes. Do you have tomato seeds?"

"I don't have tomato seeds," the store owner said, "but I do have strawberry seeds."

So Tomato Jo bought strawberry seeds, went home, and planted them in her garden. But instead of pouring water on the strawberry seeds, she poured tomato juice on them. "This way," she told herelf, "I will grow tomatoes and not straw-berries."

But she was wrong again. For when the plants grew bigger and bigger, they grew strawberries and not tomatoes.

So Tomato Jo went back to the store again. "I don't want strawberries," she said. "I want tomatoes."

"I told you they were strawberry seeds," the store owner said. "I don't have tomato seeds."

"What kind of seeds do you have?" Tomato Jo asked.

"I have blueberry seeds," the store owner said.

So Tomato Jo bought blueberry seeds, went home, planted them in her garden, and sprinkled them with tomato juice. But as the plants grew bigger and bigger, they grew blueberries, not tomatoes.

Tomato Jo didn't know this rule of life: We reap whatever we plant or sow. If we sow carrots, we reap carrots. If we sow strawberries, we reap strawberries. If we sow the wind, we reap a storm. If we sow anger, we reap anger. If we sow love, we reap love.

Wise As Solomon

Have you ever heard someone say, "That person has the wisdom of Solomon!"? Solomon, the son of King David in the Bible, was one of the wisest persons that ever lived. So when people say, "She has the wisdom of Solomon," they mean to say, "She is very, very wise."

Not many people are that wise, but the judge in our story was. He had the wisdom of Solomon. Listen!

Once upon a time there was a rich man. One day he lost his wallet. It had two thousand dollars in it. The rich man was desperate. Two thousand dollars is a lot of money—even for a rich man.

The rich man put an ad in a newspaper. It said:

LOST: A WALLET WITH TWO THOUSAND DOLLARS.
REWARD: FIVE HUNDRED DOLLARS.

Now it so happened that a poor man found the wallet. He read the ad and quickly returned the wallet to the rich man. As he handed over the wallet, he held out his hand to receive the five-hundred-dollar reward.

But the rich man thought, *Five hundred dollars is a lot of money, way too much money for this poor man.* So he asked the man, "Where is the diamond that was in the wallet?"

The poor man answered, "Diamond? What do you mean? There was no diamond in your wallet."

"Oh, yes, there was!" the rich man said. "And you took it. That's why I'm not giving you the five-hundred-dollar reward."

The poor man went to the town judge, who had the wisdom of Solomon, and told how he had been cheated.

The judge asked both the rich man and the poor man to appear in court. The judge said to the rich man, "You said your wallet had two thousand dollars and a diamond in it. There is no diamond in this wallet, so this is not your wallet. Therefore, I will let this poor man keep this wallet with two thousand dollars in it until he finds the person who lost it. Meanwhile, rich man, you keep looking for the wallet you lost with the diamond in it."

I tell you, the rich man changed his mind in a hurry and quickly gave the poor man the five-hundred-dollar reward.

Uz and Buz

Have you ever heard of Uz and Buz? If you haven't, don't feel bad. Very few people have. Very few people know who they are. So I'm going to help you find out.

Here are four different answers to the question. Only one answer is correct. See if you can guess the correct one. Are you ready?

Who are Uz and Buz?

Answer 1: Uz and Buz are two kings who lived thousands of years ago. Uz and Buz hated each other, and they fought many wars. The wars finally stopped when King Uz died in battle. In history books these wars are known as the Uz-Buz Wars.

Answer 2: Uz and Buz are two of Abraham's nephews. You remember Abraham from your Bible stories, don't you? Well, Abraham had a brother, and this brother had two sons whose names were Uz and Buz.

Answer 3: Uz and Buz are two comic-strip characters. Your grandpa and grandma will remember them. Forty or fifty years ago, Uz and Buz were as popular as Charlie Brown and Snoopy are today.

Answer 4: Uz and Buz are two crazy characters in a Dr. Seuss book. The book starts out like this: "Uz made no fuz about who he wuz."

Which of these four answers do you think is the right one? If you want to know, read Genesis 22:21.

147

Thank God for Monks

In church there are lots of Bibles. At home you probably have several Bibles. All of these Bibles are printed. Printing with letters cut from metal was invented some five hundred years ago. Since then, the Bibles we use were printed by machines. But before printing was invented, Bibles were copied by hand. Copying the books of the Bible took a very long time.

Who did all the copying of the Bible? Christian monks did. Monks, who lived in buildings called monasteries, spent hours and days and years copying the Bible. Some monks spent their whole lives copying Bibles.

Can't you imagine one monk asking another monk, "Brother John, how are you doing? Are you making any progress?"

"Very, very slowly!" John might answer. "I just finished copying the book of Genesis. Sixty-five more Bible books to go. Already I have a bad cramp in my right hand. Maybe I can finish copying the whole Bible in two years. Then I'll probably start on a new copy of the Bible."

Monasteries were not heated in those days. In winter they were the coldest places on earth. Even so, monks kept on carefully copying the Bible unless, of course, the ink in the inkwells froze solid.

When monks finished copying a Bible, they sometimes scribbled notes at the end. One monk wrote, "The end of the book. Thanks be to God." Another monk wrote, "Pray that God will bless my soul and God will bless your soul."

Next time you pick up a Bible—a Bible printed by machine—think of the monks who copied Bibles by hand. Then thank God for them. If it hadn't been for them, you wouldn't have a Bible today.

How Much Land?

L eo Tolstoy, a Russian writer, wrote many beautiful stories. One of his stories is about a man called Pakhom. Let me tell you the story.

Pakhom is a farmer who has but one wish—to have more land. One day Pakhom hears that in the country of the Bashkirs there is plenty of land available at a cheap price. So he goes there and talks to the Bashkir chief. "What is your price for the land?" Pakhom asks.

"Only a thousand dollars a day," the chief answers.

"How many acres would that be?" Pakhom asks.

"We don't sell by the acre," the chief answers. "We sell only by the day. As much land as you can walk around in a day, that much land is yours. That's the way we figure land, and the price is one thousand dollars a day.

"But let me warn you. If on that same day you do not return to the spot where you started, you lose your thousand dollars."

"It's a deal," Pakhom says.

The next day before sunrise Pakhom and his servant and the Bashkir chief with some of his men go to a hill over-looking a vast area of grassland. The chief takes off his cap, lays it down, and says, "This will be the mark. Lay your money in the cap and have your servant remain beside it while you are gone. From this mark you will start and to this mark you will return."

(Adapted from Leo Tolstoy's short story entitled, "How Much Land Does a Man Need?")

Pakhom takes out his money, lays it in the cap, and then starts walking toward the east. A couple of mounted Bashkirs ride behind him to drive in stakes to mark off Pakhom's land.

After walking a couple of miles, Pakhom grows warm and takes off some of his clothes. Later, Pakhom takes off his boots. *Walking without them will be easier,* he tells himself. On and on he walks—for the farther he goes, the better the land becomes.

Pakhom begins to tire. Glancing at the sun, he sees that it's time for lunch. He eats some bread but without sitting down. Having eaten, he feels strong again. And on he goes.

The sun seems to grow hotter and hotter. Pakhom is almost worn out. As he is about to begin to return to the spot where he started, he sees another section of beautiful land. He decides he must have it, so he walks on.

It's getting late now, and Pakhom has to be back before sunset. So he finally heads for the starting point. *I must hurry straight back now, otherwise I won't make it back in time,* Pakhom tells himself.

Pakhom's feet are aching and from time to time he staggers. But he still has a long way to go. To make it back in time, Pakhom breaks into a run. He can hear the Bashkirs cheering him on. Now he can see the cap and his servant sitting beside it. Pakhom reaches the hill just as the red sun touches the earth. He scrambles up the slope. Then he stumbles and falls. As he falls, he stretches out his hand toward the cap and touches it.

"Pakhom, you have earned much land indeed!" the Bashkir chief shouts.

But Pakhom does not hear. When his servant tries to raise him, he finds that Pakhom is dead.

After a while the chief gets up, takes a spade from the ground, throws it to Pakhom's servant, and says, "Bury him!"

After the Bashkirs have left, the servant buries his master in a small plot of land—just big enough for his master's body.

Poor Pakhom was a greedy man. He thought, *The more land I have, the happier I'll be.*

But Jesus says, "What kind of deal is it to get all the land you want but lose your life?"

It Comes with the Ticket

The story I'm about to tell you really happened. It happened about eighty-five years ago.

A poor family living in Europe heard that things were a lot better in North America. So they saved every penny they could to buy tickets for a ship to America. They saved for years. Finally they had enough money to buy the tickets.

When they boarded the ship, all they had were the clothes they wore and a few loaves of bread and some cheese. That's all. For three days the family ate only cheese sandwiches. Finally the little girl in the family had had quite enough of it. She said, "I hate cheese sandwiches! If that's all I have to eat, I'm going to die before I reach America."

The father, feeling sorry for his daughter, gave her his last nickel. "Here," he said, "go buy yourself an ice-cream cone in the dining room."

The little girl disappeared and didn't return for a long time. The father was getting worried.

At last the girl showed up. She had a full stomach and a big smile on her face. "Where were you all that time?" her father asked.

"In the dining room, getting something to eat."

"What did you eat?"

"Three ice-cream cones. Then I was still hungry so I had a steak dinner."

"You bought all that with a nickel?" her father asked.

(Adapted from Peter Kreeft, *Fundamentals of the Faith* [Harrison, NY: Ignatius Press, 1988], 142.)

"Oh, no. Here's your nickel. The food is free. It comes with the ticket."

About five hundred years ago people thought that they had to pay God to have God forgive their sins. They thought that the more money they paid, the more sins God would forgive. And the more good works they did, the more sins God would forgive.

Then came Martin Luther, who said, "Forgiveness is free. God gives forgiveness to those who believe in Jesus. Forgiveness comes with faith. Forgiveness comes with the ticket of faith."

The Chocolate Boy

Once upon a time there was a boy about your age. What was special about this boy was that he was made of chocolate. Whether he was born a chocolate boy or had become one later, he could not remember. The only thing he knew for sure was that he was made of chocolate.

Now this chocolate boy had one weakness—the same weakness you have. He liked chocolate. He liked chocolate in the morning, afternoon, and evening.

One day, when there wasn't a crumb of chocolate in the house and when he didn't have any money to buy chocolate, he looked at his fingers and said, "Hey, I never noticed it before, but I have two of each kind of fingers. I have two thumbs, two index fingers, two middle fingers, two ring fingers, and two pinkies. I don't need two of each. I can easily get along with one of each." So he ate his right pinkie. Mmmmmm! Did that taste good!

His piano teacher was the first to notice. "Why are you skipping all the high notes?" she asked. She looked at his right hand and saw that his pinkie was missing.

From that day on the chocolate boy decided not to eat any more of his fingers. He decided to eat his toes instead.

But missing toes are a problem, too. Toes help us keep our balance. When we're missing a couple of toes, we easily lose our balance. And that's what happened to the chocolate boy. Because he had eaten a couple of his toes, he would often stumble and fall.

(Adapted from John R. Aurelio, *Fables for God's People* [New York: Crossroad, 1988], 57–58.)

Still, he could not leave his own chocolate alone. He kept eating away at himself. By the time he finished high school, he had eaten all his toes. And by the time he finished college, he had eaten his right foot and his left hand. That he made it through college was nothing short of a miracle.

After college he learned to cut down on chocolate. Still, he liked himself so much, he kept eating himself until at last the only part of his body that was left was his hungry mouth.

People who like themselves so much that all they do is talk about themselves are like that chocolate boy. They love themselves so much that they don't have any love left for others. Their mouths are filled with themselves, and they only enjoy the taste of themselves. And they eat themselves until there is nothing left, nothing but a hungry mouth.

Good and Bad Manners

Some time ago I read an interesting book. It was written more than 150 years ago by Samuel Miller, a seminary professor. Samuel Miller complained about the bad manners of many ministers.

Here are five of his complaints:

Complaint 1: Many ministers chew tobacco, and from time to time they spit on the living-room carpet of the people they visit.

If you had been living 150 years ago and if your dad had said, "Let's ask the minister to come and visit us," your mom would have said, "Are you crazy? We just bought a new carpet. The minister will spit on it and ruin it."

Complaint 2: Many ministers smoke so much that people hate to sit next to them. People complain that their clothes smell like smoke.

If you had been living 150 years ago, your dad might have come home from a meeting in church and said, "Guess what? I sat next to the minister all night." And your mom would have said, "You don't have to tell me that. I can smell it."

Complaint 3: Many ministers laugh so loud that you can hear them through the whole house and even in the street. People walking by a house would say, "Our minister must be visiting here. Hear that loud laugh?"

Complaint 4: Many ministers clean their nails with a knife in public and comb their hair in public. Then they clean the comb while everybody watches.

Complaint 5: Some ministers pick their teeth while sitting at the dinner table. If you have to pick your teeth at all, Samuel

Miller writes in his book, "Cover your mouth with a hand-kerchief. And be sure never to pick your teeth with your fork."

I enjoyed reading Samuel Miller's book. But I have one question: Why pick on ministers? Why should only ministers have good manners? Why shouldn't everyone have good manners? Just because you aren't a minister doesn't mean that you can spit on someone's carpet or laugh too loud in company or clean your nails in public or pick your teeth at the table.

Agree?

The Fisherman's Wish

Once, long ago and far away, so an old story goes, there was a poor fisherman who lived in a hut. He owned only a leaky rowboat, a fishnet, a stew pot, and two wooden bowls.

One day he caught a large fish. To his great surprise, the fish talked. It said, "Please, don't kill me. If you let me go free, wish for anything you want and I will give it to you."

"It's a deal," the fisherman said, and he asked for seven gold coins. One to pay someone to fix his leaky boat. One to buy two porcelain soup bowls. Two to buy two silver spoons. One to buy himself some new clothes. And two to buy some beautiful presents for his wife.

But if you think these seven gold coins made the fisherman happy, you're wrong. After he had spent the seven coins, he wished he had asked for a hundred gold coins so he could buy a nice cottage.

So the fisherman went back to the place where he had caught the fish and shouted:

"Fish of the sea,
please come around
and listen to me!"

No sooner had he shouted these words than the fish came swimming toward him.

"What is it you want?" it asked.

The fisherman said, "My wife and I are sick and tired of living in a hut. We want to live in a nice cottage."

"Your wish has been granted," the fish said. "Go home to

your new cottage."

But if you think this new cottage made the fisherman and his wife happy, you're wrong again. After a couple of months they said to each other, "This cottage is getting too small for us. If only we could live in a bigger place, we would be happy."

So the fisherman went back to the place where he had caught the fish and shouted:

"Fish of the sea,
please come around
and listen to me!"

No sooner had he shouted these words than the fish came swimming toward him and asked, "What is it you want?" And the fisherman said, "My wife and I would like to live in a mansion."

"Your wish has been granted," the fish said. "Go home to your mansion."

But if you think that the mansion made the fisherman and his wife happy, you are wrong once more. After a couple of months they looked at each other and said, "Wouldn't it be nice to live in an even bigger place? Wouldn't it be nice to live in a castle?"

So the fisherman went back to the place where he had caught the fish and shouted:

"Fish of the sea,
please come around
and listen to me!"

No sooner had he shouted these words than the fish came swimming toward him and asked, "What is it you want this time?"

"My wife and I want to live in a castle," the fisherman said.

"Your wish has been granted," the fish said. "Go home to your castle."

When the fisherman came home to his castle, he said to his wife, "Now we will live happily ever after!" But a couple of months later the fisherman said to his wife, "Wouldn't it be nice if I were to be king—king of the castle?"

"It surely would," his wife said. "Why don't you ask the fish to grant your wish?"

And the fish did. It granted the wish. And it granted many more wishes. But the fisherman and his wife were never satisfied. They lived unhappily ever after.

No wonder. For it is as Jesus says, "The more you have, the easier it is to forget me. And when you forget me, you soon become unhappy, even though you may be king of the castle."

Watch Out for Flatterers

Once upon a time there was a fox. One day, as this fox was sitting around doing nothing, he smelled something.

"Does my nose smell rightly?" the fox asked himself. "Am I smelling cheese? Yes, I am."

So the fox followed his nose, which was smelling cheese, until he came to a big tree. The fox looked up and saw a crow sitting on a branch and holding in its beak a piece of cheese.

The fox thought, *That piece of cheese is in the wrong mouth. It belongs in my mouth, not in the crow's mouth. If I don't get that piece of cheese, I will be the most unhappy animal in the entire forest. But how can I get it? Maybe by flattery?*

So the fox said to the crow, "Crow, has anyone ever told you how handsome you are? Has anyone ever told you what beautiful feathers you have? Let me tell you something, Crow. If your voice is as beautiful as your feathers, then you are the most beautiful bird of the forest."

Wow! the crow thought. *No one has ever said such nice things about me before, not even my own mother.* And to show that its voice was just as beautiful as its feathers, the crow opened its beak to sing and . . . dropped the piece of cheese.

The fox quickly ate the cheese and then said, "Crow, you fell for my flattering words. Did you really think I meant what I said? No, sirree! All I wanted was that piece of cheese. Good-bye!"

Never trust a flattering mouth, the Bible says. Watch out for people who flatter you. All they want is your cheese.

Flood-the-Building Sunday

Ministers get a lot of strange mail. One of the strangest pieces of mail I ever received was a catalog selling things to churches. One thing listed in the catalog was a Super Squirt Gun. The catalog said, "Why not have a Flood-the-Building Sunday? Why not give each child that attends church school a Super Squirt Gun? And why not let the children who bring visitors to church-school class squirt the teacher in the face?"

After I read that, I had a much better idea. *At the end of the church-school year,* I thought, *why not ask all church-school teachers to come forward and line up in front of the pulpit? Then why not ask all church-school children to come forward with their loaded Super Squirt Guns and squirt their teachers in the face? That would be a way to say, "Thank you for teaching me."*

Come to think of it, I have an even better idea. Once a year, when a number of elders and deacons retire, why not ask them to come forward and line up in front of the pulpit? Then why not hand out loaded Super Squirt Guns to all the church members and ask them to come forward and squirt the elders and deacons in the face, as a way of saying, "Thank you for serving God as elders and deacons"? Then we'd really have a Flood-the-Building Sunday.

Do you know what this church catalog reminds me of? Of the story of Jesus cleansing the temple.

One day Jesus entered the temple and knocked over all the tables of the money changers so that money went flying in all directions.

Now, if there had been a table piled high with Super

Squirt Guns selling for twenty-five cents each, I'm quite sure Jesus would have knocked over that table too. Super Squirt Guns would have been flying in all directions.

That's what I think. What do you think?

Long Necks

Let me ask you a question: Have you ever seen an ostrich swallow an apple? It's not at all like watching your cat swallow a piece of meat. Your cat's meat goes down so fast you can almost hear it hit the cat's stomach.

But an ostrich has a long neck. When it swallows an apple, the apple takes a long time to get to the ostrich's stomach.

Let me ask you another question: Have you ever seen a giraffe swallow a watermelon? It's not at all like watching your friend swallow a cookie. Your friend's cookie goes down so fast you can almost hear it hit the bottom of her stomach.

But a giraffe has a very long neck. When a giraffe swallows a watermelon, the melon takes a very long time to get down to the giraffe's stomach. I suppose a giraffe has to eat breakfast in the evening and lunch first thing in the morning in order for those meals to reach its stomach on time.

Let me ask you one more question: Don't you think that sometimes you are just like an ostrich or a giraffe? You're not? But sometimes I wonder.

When your mom or dad tells you to clean your messy room and you say, "Okay!" do you wait a day before you begin cleaning up? If you do, you're just like an ostrich or a giraffe. You swallow your mom's or dad's words, but the words take a long time to go down your long neck and do any good.

Some way or other you have to get rid of that long neck of yours.

Words Like Arrows

Words are more than sounds. Words can be like arrows. They can hurt others deeply. Have you ever used a bow and arrow? You must hold the bow, put the arrow in place, pull back the string, carefully aim the arrow, and then shoot it. What happens? The arrow travels to its target, hits it, and enters it.

There is a story in the Bible about two men, Jehu and Joram. Joram was trying to escape from Jehu. But Jehu drew his bow with all his strength, carefully aimed his arrow, and shot Joram between the shoulders so that the arrow entered Joram's heart.

Now think of words as arrows. You make words with your mouth, aim the words at someone, and then let go of them. What happens? Your words travel through the air, hit the person you're talking to, and enter that person. When you say to your brother or sister, "You're stupid!" your words travel through the air, hit your brother or sister, and enter their lives.

That's a scary business, isn't it? There's something scary about words. Once you say them, once you let words leave your mouth, you can't call them back. You can't say, "Come back, words! Back into my mouth!" Just as Jehu couldn't call back the arrow he shot at Joram after it had left his bow, so you can't call back words after they leave your lips. Once an arrow is on its way, you no longer have control over it. Once words are on their way, you no longer have control over them. So guard your lips, the Bible warns. Make sure that the words that leave your mouth won't harm anyone.

More Great Story Sermons for Children

Once Upon a Time...
Story Sermons for Children
John Timmer

If you've found the story sermons in *How Long Is God's Nose?* helpful in your ministry, look for John Timmer's first book of story sermons, *Once Upon a Time....* This collection of 102 stories brings truth to life for children through imaginative ideas and delightful language.

Once Upon a Time... is available at your local Christian bookstore.

ZondervanPublishingHouse
Grand Rapids, Michigan
http://www.zondervan.com

A Division of HarperCollinsPublishers

We want to hear from you. Please send your comments about this
book to us in care of the address below. Thank you.

ZondervanPublishingHouse

Grand Rapids, Michigan 49530

http://www.zondervan.com